Battle Orders • 38

Panzer Divisions
1944–45

Pier Paolo Battistelli

Consultant Editor Dr Duncan Anderson • *Series editors* Marcus Cowper and Nikolai Bogdanovic

First published in Great Britain in 2009 by Osprey Publishing, Midland House, West Way, Botley, Oxford OX2 0PH, United Kingdom.
Email: info@ospreypublishing.com

Print ISBN 978 1 84603 406 0
PDF e-book ISBN 978 1 84908 084 2

Editorial by Ilios Publishing, Oxford, UK (www.iliospublishing.com)
Design and cartography: Bounford.com
Index by Alan Thatcher
Originated by United Graphics Pte
Printed and bound in China through Bookbuilders

09 10 11 12 13   10 9 8 7 6 5 4 3 2 1
A CIP catalogue record for this book is available from the British Library.

For a catalogue of all books published by Osprey Military and Aviation please contact:
Osprey Direct USA, c/o Random House Distribution Center, 400 Hahn Rd, Westminster, MD 21157 USA
E-mail: uscustomerservice@ospreypublishing.com

Osprey Direct, The Book Service Ltd, Distribution Centre, Colchester Road, Frating Green, Colchester, Essex, CO7 7DW, UK
E-mail: customerservice@ospreypublishing.com

Osprey Publishing is supporting the Woodland Trust, the UK's leading woodland conservation charity by funding the dedication of trees.

www.ospreypublishing.com

Acknowledgements

The author wishes to thank: Nik Cornish, Antonio Attarantato and Carlo Pecchi for the photographs, Mr. Andrew Orgill and the staff of the Central Library, Royal Military Academy Sandhurst, Dr. Christopher Pugsley and Dr. Klaus Schmider (Department of War Studies, Royal Military Academy Sandhurst) for their friendly help and support and, last but not least, the series editors Marcus Cowper and Nikolai Bogdanovic.

Author's note

In the tree diagrams and maps in this volume, the units and movements of national forces are depicted in the following colours:

German Army units	Grey
Waffen-SS units	Black
Luftwaffe units	Blue
Soviet units	Red
US units	Green
British and Canadian units	Brown

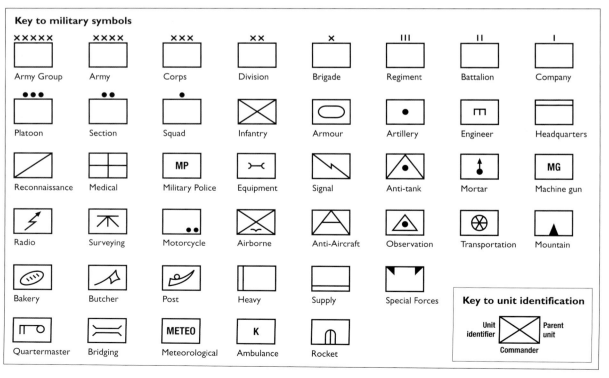

Key to military symbols

Army Group, Army, Corps, Division, Brigade, Regiment, Battalion, Company

Platoon, Section, Squad, Infantry, Armour, Artillery, Engineer, Headquarters

Reconnaissance, Medical, Military Police, Equipment, Signal, Anti-tank, Mortar, Machine gun

Radio, Surveying, Motorcycle, Airborne, Anti-Aircraft, Observation, Transportation, Mountain

Bakery, Butcher, Post, Heavy, Supply, Special Forces

Quartermaster, Bridging, Meteorological, Ambulance, Rocket

Key to unit identification

Unit identifier, Parent unit, Commander

Contents

Introduction

Following the failure of the Kursk offensive, the German Army fought on the defensive, first on the Eastern Front, then in Italy and on the Western Front. The nature of warfare had changed again after the victorious years, and the German Army adapted to meet the new requirements. Even the Panzerwaffe, the German armoured force that once spearheaded the blitzkrieg campaigns, changed its methods of operation. In turn, the role of the Panzer Divisions changed, as they found themselves called upon to fight defensive battles. No longer were there armoured thrusts into enemy territory; those that did happen served only to relieve encircled units and allow them to escape. Tank battles were now mainly fought to prevent the enemy from breaking through the German defence lines. Furthermore, since late 1943 the Panzer Divisions of the Heer (Army) no longer represented the sole component of the Panzerwaffe; new Waffen-SS Panzer Divisions were upgraded or raised, while small armoured units, like the heavy Tiger tank battalions, acquired greater importance.

Yet the Panzer Divisions still made up the bulk of the Panzerwaffe; understrength, outnumbered and often fighting alone for months on end, they faced the Soviet offensives on the Eastern Front and later spearheaded the German forces both in Italy and in Normandy, eventually matching the role of their Waffen-SS counterparts. Both served as 'firefighters' on the most threatened areas of the front, as did other Panzer units such as the Tiger tank battalions. Somehow, the role played by Army Panzer Divisions was less glamorous and often comprised involvement in unknown battles fought in unknown places. However, while the Waffen-SS could be called in at given places and times, the Army Panzer Divisions still formed the backbone of the German armed forces, despite their progressive weakening. In fact the overall reorganization of the Panzerwaffe, started before Kursk, failed to restore their overall potential and instead merely produced some high-quality divisions. Although a lack of balance was not new in the Panzer Divisions, a new factor further weakened their combat effectiveness: the dispersion of forces.

On paper, the 1943 and 1944 Panzer Divisions were stronger than ever; new tanks, a larger allotment of armoured vehicles for infantry and other units, self-propelled artillery and a new generation of tank hunters provided them with a firepower no one would have dreamt of just a few years before. However, only a few divisions ever came to be fully reorganized according to the intended establishments, and many others fought relentlessly still equipped with the same tanks, vehicles and weapons they had been using in early 1943. Lack of supplies, in particular fuel (which greatly hampered their combat capabilities), all too often reduced them to the status of a small Kampfgruppe, a battle group formed around the few armoured and motorized units. Nonetheless, these divisions were irreplaceable in their defensive roles and, as a result, reorganization only affected the newly raised ones and (to a certain extent) those that had been badly mauled and refitted. Yet, in spite of their overall poor shape, these divisions fought on all the fronts and still proved capable of hitting back and spreading havoc amongst their enemies. As the Ardennes offensive of December 1944 proved, the Panzerwaffe was still able to drive deep into enemy-held territory. However, this time the enemy had changed.

A PzKpfw V Panther Ausf D seeks cover somewhere in the battlefields of Italy; once positioned, it will start firing against enemy targets. The only Panther-equipped army unit to see action in this theatre of war was the I./Panzer Regiment 4, detached from the 13. to the 26. Panzer Division.

Combat mission

Although the German Army was forced onto the defensive in the summer of 1943, its leading principles of warfare remained unchanged; attack, or counterattack, was still the best way of achieving results against enemy forces. Facing more enemies and fighting on several fronts simultaneously, the German Army found in the Panzer Divisions a suitable instrument for a makeshift solution: counterattacking enemy strikes when and where these took place. Until 1944 German doctrine envisaged a linear defence based on a main defence line, to be held at all costs regardless of enemy breakthroughs. Mobile forces, above all the Panzer Divisions, were then ordered to counterattack, surround and eventually destroy the enemy forces and restore the situation. Such a system, which worked well on the Eastern Front until mid-1944, had several shortcomings, however; in order to face enemy attacks which threatened if not all at least good portions of the front, the Panzer Divisions had to be scattered all along it because the lack of reserves and supplies did not permit the switching of units fast enough to face the impending crisis. This led to the exact opposite of one of the leading principles of German warfare: the concentration of forces. As a result, the Germans could still deal locally with enemy breakthroughs and restore the situation (though often with severe losses), but they were no longer able to regain the initiative and launch any major offensives.

The crew of a PzKpfw IV Ausf H looking out for the approaching enemy; the tank features all the late-war improvements, which include hull and turret skirts (Schürzen) and the anti-magnetic mine paste on the hull, known as 'Zimmerit'. The low-visibility numbers are also worth noting.

Eventually, a lack of strength and resources led to the defence in depth concept. Since the enemy relied heavily on firepower, the forward defensive line was thinned down and comprised only a series of outposts intended to slow down the enemy attacking forces, while a main line of resistance was built in the rear. When the enemy attack came, the Panzer Divisions had to contain their drives and eventually counterattack following the usual guidelines. Once again that led to a dispersion of forces and, as a result, no major offensive was possible – as witnessed in Normandy. The debate between Rommel and Von Rundstedt about the deployment of the Panzer Divisions clearly reflects the situation; Rommel fully acknowledged Allied air superiority and its impact on the Panzer Divisions' operational capabilities, while Von Rundstedt was seeking to regain the initiative through the concentration of forces and a major offensive. Worth noting, both men were right in their points of view; as the Ardennes offensive of December 1944 was to show, only a concentration of forces that managed to seek out a Schwerpunkt – a 'central gravity point' – against the weaker enemy positions could generate a breakthrough that might eventually lead to the surrounding and destruction of enemy forces and the regaining of the initiative.

The fact that the Ardennes offensive took advantage of bad weather to deny enemy air superiority does, on the other hand, show that Rommel was also right. In fact, during the closing years of the war the Panzerwaffe was compelled to wage war in a way for which it was not suited – i.e. a defensive war which mainly sought to gain time or to hold ground rather than to seek out a decisive victory on the field through manoeuvre. The Ardennes offensive was a doomed one, but it was the last attempt made to try to put into practice the lessons of German armoured warfare doctrine. When this was done, the odds were so unfavourable that success never came within reach of the Panzer Divisions, even though they proved again that they were still capable of demonstrating mastery of the battlefield.

Doctrine and training

Close cooperation between the Panzers and the Panzergrenadiers increased towards the end of the war. The armament of this group of Panzergrenadiers includes the new assault rifle Sturmgewehr 44, which indicates that they are part of a company's Sturm Zug in action during the closing months of war.

There was no major change in German armour doctrine in the closing years of the war, only adaptations to the terrain and to new weapons and equipment. In 1943 the Panzer Regiment, or sometimes the Panzer Abteilung, was the leading unit around which the main Kampfgruppe (combat group) was built. In the closing stages of the war many divisions were able to create fully armoured Kampfgruppen that included elements of Panzer, Panzergrenadier, Pionier, Panzerjäger, artillery and other support units. It was employed like a miniature Panzer Division, following the same rules of armoured doctrine; Panzer units led the way, breaking through the enemy defences and were closely supported by self-propelled Artillerie, while follow-up infantry, supported by Panzerjäger and Pionier units, secured the area and defended the flanks of the armoured drive. Although it remained in use until 1945, this doctrine underwent several changes caused by new factors encountered on the battle front.

First there were the new tactics of the Red Army, based on the creation of an anti-tank defence screen to meet German armoured counterattacks; since Panzer units could no longer afford huge losses, the infantry was now required to deal directly with the anti-tank screen while the Panzers manoeuvred against the enemy spearheads, often with the support of the Panzer Aufklärungs Abteilung. This was now rarely used in its traditional reconnaissance role and, because of its organization, was instead used as a regular combat unit. Another decisive factor was Allied air superiority and firepower, which had a considerable impact on German armoured doctrine. While on the Eastern Front it was still possible to group large numbers of forces, in Italy (where Allied naval support was so deadly) and in North-West Europe this was no longer possible, since these large groups would have fallen prey to enemy air forces and artillery. Therefore, the Panzer units no longer spearheaded the leading Kampfgruppe but were rather split into smaller, company-sized units and used to support the Panzergrenadier and the Panzer Aufklärungs units. The Kampfgruppe became smaller, and doctrine returned to infiltration tactics, aimed at achieving modest breakthroughs followed by swift advances. The most logical consequence of this change was smaller, no longer decisive, breakthroughs which had little impact.

Counterattacking enemy breakthroughs, which included Allied beachheads both in Italy and in Normandy, was one of the main tasks of the Panzer Divisions. Here a Sturmgeschütz III, which could equip both the Panzer and the Panzerjäger Abteilung, is moving past a destroyed Sherman tank.

From 1943 onwards, both the Panzerkorps (armoured corps) and the Panzerarmee (armoured army) were armoured only in name. They turned into a mixture of armoured and non-armoured units which, though well-suited to defence, lacked the necessary make-up for major offensive actions. The need for closer cooperation between the Panzer Divisions and the others, imposed by defensive needs, added further limitations to the former. The battle for Normandy offers a perfect example; in spite of the concentration of armoured forces achieved in the area, hardly any Panzer Divisions were grouped together to launch a major counterattack; indeed, since the lack of forces led to their deployment on the front line, they were denied the advantages of mobility and speed. Though still quite effective in defence, as the battles on the German border showed, the Panzer Divisions had clearly lost the edge.

This was despite their increased firepower, which was greater than ever. The new Panther tank, though slow to be delivered, provided Panzer units for the first time with a tank that greatly outmatched its Allied counterparts and dealt with the Soviet equivalents on a even footing. Even anti-tank defences were improved thanks to new anti-tank weapons like the Panzerschreck

and the Panzerfaust and to the new Jagdpanzer, which replaced the old Panzerjäger with an all-round, heavily armoured gun carrier. The latter eventually brought about changes in German doctrine; turretless, self-propelled gun carriers like the Sturmgeschütz and the new Jagdpanzer became offensive weapons, though they now required closer cooperation with the infantry. However, due to enemy air superiority movement was now mainly confined to night-time or favourable weather, and anti-aircraft artillery (often self-propelled) was also required at every level – the presence of which further limited the divisions' speed and mobility.

Last but not least, during the last two years of war the Panzer Divisions also faced a major training crisis. The heavy personnel losses of the previous years, plus those suffered during the summer of 1944, could only partly be made good using newly recruited personnel, and when this did happen divisional and unit commanders discovered that replacements needed a lot of additional training before joining their experienced, battle-hardened comrades in arms. The Feld Ersatz Bataillon (the divisional field replacement battalion) allowed replacements to complete their training along with personnel from the division; this not only refined their skills (for example in the use of heavy weapons and of artillery), but also helped the recruits to acquaint themselves with battlefront conditions. Technical training required by Panzer, Aufklärungs and Pionier units, on the other hand, meant that these units were sent back to Germany to refit and reorganize. Moreover, in 1944–45 the Germans faced serious problems due to a shortage of trained officers and non-commissioned officers, which could only be made good by promoting from the ranks. The situation became particularly troublesome during the last, major reorganization in autumn 1944, in spite of the overall, dramatic, reduction in strength imposed by the new tables of organization.

All these problems notwithstanding, it is worth noting that even during the difficult last year of war the Panzer Divisions performed well, often better than their Waffen-SS counterparts, and – as the Ardennes offensive was eventually to show – they still could achieve some decisive results.

Although the last models were produced in August 1943, the PzKpfw III remained in use (though not with frontline units) until the end of the war. Here we see a trainload of PzKpfw IV Ausf G tanks, including some PzKpfw III Ausf M; with the November 1943 establishment, these were still part of the Panzer Abteilung's Stabskompanie.

A Panzergrenadier veteran Oberfeldwebel (technical sergeant) in a training camp in Germany, in a staged propaganda photo. Other than a 'wound' badge, he displays the iron crosses first and second class, the infantry assault badge and the close combat badge. Such experienced men were essential for training and leading the new recruits.

Unit organization

From 1943 to 1944

An order of the German Army High Command of 24 September 1943 introduced a common organization structure for all the Panzer Divisions (with the exception of 21. Panzer and Panzer Division Norwegen) which, minor variations apart, matched that already introduced in June for the Panzer Divisions taking part in Operation *Zitadelle*. It was in practice a mere acknowledgement of the status quo, since no overall reorganization was possible due to the lack of men and equipment; nonetheless, on 1 November 1943 a new series of war establishment charts (KStN) were issued for the '1943 Panzer Division' organization. This was to have a total strength of 16,385 all ranks (439 officers, 89 officials, 3,781 NCOs, 12,076 ORs – 961 of which could be replaced by foreign auxiliaries, the Hiwi – plus 800 replacements in the Feldersatz Bataillon) armed with 10,808 rifles, 1,818 MPs, 695 light and 103 heavy MGs, 36 medium and 14 heavy mortars, 25 anti-tank guns plus 174 Panzerschreck, 25 field and four infantry guns and howitzers, eight 88mm and 38 20mm anti-aircraft guns (self-propelled ones not included), 771 cars, 1,946 lorries, 226 non-armoured half-tracks, 662 motorcycles, 215 tanks (of which 99

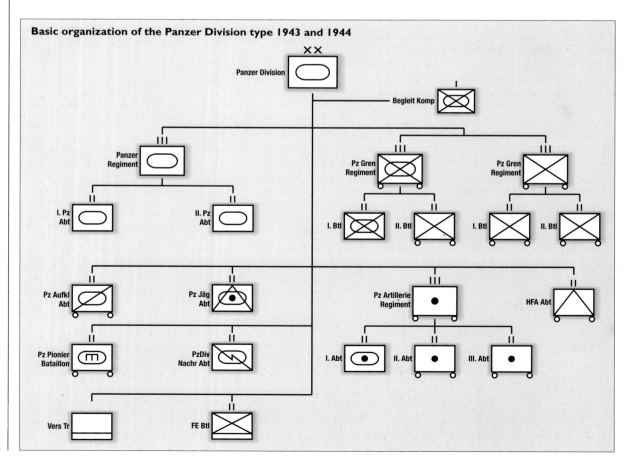

Basic organization of the Panzer Division type 1943 and 1944

were Panther tanks and 98 PzKpfw IV), 45 Panzerjäger and 405 AFVs, including 37 self-propelled guns of all types, 39 half-track mounted Flak guns, almost 300 armoured half-tracks (233 SdKfz 251 and 64 SdKfz 250) and 32 armoured cars. In practice not a single division in the field matched its paper establishment, chiefly because most of the PzKpfw V Panther-equipped Panzer Abteilungen were still forming.

Also foreseeing the availability of new weapons, on 1 April 1944 the new '1944 Panzer Division' organization was thus introduced, though the KStN were still being issued in July. Actually, between April and May 1944 several Panzer Divisions were meant to be reorganized, but only a few of them actually completed the process before being committed to the front. On 3 August 1944 all divisions (except 21. Panzer and Panzer Lehr Division) were ordered to begin reorganizing using available equipment and personnel, while reporting on their status to allow for the issue of needed weapons and replacements. Overall organization of the '1944 Panzer Division' still matched that of the 1943 version, and changes mainly took place at regimental and battalion level. First and foremost the new 'freie Gliederung' (free organization) was introduced, which saw the creation for every battalion of a supply company (Versorgungs Kompanie) from the supply units and trains of every company. Since the commander of the Versorgungs Kompanie was also deputy battalion commander, the new organization enabled the latter to focus exclusively on combat duties, while the former took exclusive care of any logistical and administrative needs.

Other changes affected overall strength and equipment; most notably, infantry units lost their many anti-tank platoons, while heavy mortar and flamethrower platoons were introduced. The overall strength of the 1944 Panzer Division was 14,053 (411 officers, 85 Beamten, 3,219 NCOs, 10,338 ORs with 686 Hiwi plus 800 replacements) with 9,103 rifles, 1,637 MPs, 768 light and 98 heavy MGs, 16 medium and 18 heavy mortars, 13 anti-tank guns and 9 Panzerschreck, 25 field guns and howitzers, eight 88mm, 36 20mm and six 37mm Flak guns, 303 cars, 852 lorries, 95 half-tracks and 171 motorcycles plus 179 tanks (79 Panther, 81 PzKpfw IV, eight Flakpanzer and 11 command and recovery tanks), 31 Panzerjäger and 372 AFVs, including 16 half-track mounted Flak guns, 36 gun carriers, about 300 armoured half-tracks (245 SdKfz 251 and 59 SdKfz 250) and 16 armoured cars, all heavy. Even such a noticeable reduction failed to close the growing gap between availability and need, further exacerbated by the heavy losses suffered during the summer, and the overall lack of manpower and equipment. Therefore, on 1 November 1944 new KStN were issued leading to the late 1944 Panzer Division organization, which only affected Panzer and Panzergrenadier regiments plus the Panzer Aufklärungs and Panzerjäger Abteilung. The overall strength now dropped to 13,067 (416 officers, 77 Beamten, 2,964 NCOs, 9,610 ORs, 629 Hiwi, 800 replacements) with 8,719 rifles and 270 Sturmgewehr 44, 1,527 MPs, 574 light and 32 heavy MGs, 12 medium

A PzKpfw V Panther Ausf D on the battlefield. Many considered it to be not only Germany's best tank, but also one of the best in the world. This version weighed 43 tons, had a maximum speed of 45 kilometres per hour (25/30 off-road) and a range of 200 kilometres on road (100 off-road); its armour was on average 80mm thick.

Table 1: 1943 Panzer Division

Personnel				Weapons			
Offs	**Beamten**	**NCOs**	**ORs (Hiwi)**	**Rifles**	**MPs**	**LMG (HMG)**	**Mortars (heavy)**
Divisions Kommando (with Divisions Kartenstelle and Begleit Kompanie)							
25	10	68	257 (17)	228	22	15 (2)	2
(+)4 x SdKfz 10/4							
Panzer Regiment							
63	9	880	1,466 (170)	1,004	296	46	
(+) 6 x SdKfz 7/1 / 6 x SdKfz 251/7 / 4 x SdKfz 251/8							
(1 x PzKpfw III / 2 x PzKpfw III PzBefh / 7 x SdKfz 141 (Pz III Flamm) / 99 x Panther / 98 x PzKpfw IV)							
Panzergrenadier Regiment (gepanzert, with 9–11. Kompanie)							
61	7	556	1,997 (84)	1,599	438	149 (35)	8 (4)
(+) 6 x SdKfz 138/1 / 37 x SdKfz 251/1 / 6 x SdKfz 251/2 / 20 x SdKfz 251/3 / 5 x SdKfz 251/4 / 6 x SdKfz 251/7 / 1 x SdKfz 251/8 / 12 x SdKfz 251/9 / 4 x SdKfz 251/10 / 7 x SdKfz 251/11 / 6 x SdKfz 251/16 / 22 x SdKfz 251/17 / 12 x SdKfz 10/4							
Panzergrenadier Regiment (motorisiert, with 9–11. Kompanie)							
57	6	503	1,947 (87)	1,585	281	149 (44)	14 (8)
(+) 6 x SdKfz 138/1 / 2 x ACs SdKfz 261 / 3 x SdKfz 251/1 / 1 x SdKfz 251/3 / 1 x SdKfz 251/11 / 12 x SdKfz 10/4							
Panzer Aufklärungs Abteilung							
26	3	279	765 (34)	622	189	49 (4)	2
(+) 12 x SdKfz 222 / 6 x SdKfz 223 / 3 x SdKfz 231 / 3 x SdKfz 232 / 6 x SdKfz 233 / 22 x SdKfz 250/1 / 2 x SdKfz 250/3 / 9 x SdKfz 250/5 / 4 x SdKfz 250/7 / 3 x SdKfz 250/8 / 16 x SdKfz 250/9 / 6 x SdKfz 251/1 / 11 x SdKfz 251/3 / 7 x SdKfz 251/7 / 1 x SdKfz 251/8 / 6 x SdKfz 251/9 / 3 x SdKfz 251/11 / 4 x SdKfz 251/17							
Panzerjäger Abteilung							
18	3	207	422 (43)	330	75	4	
(+) 3 x SdKfz 7/1 / 1x SdKfz 251/8 45 x Panzerjäger (Marder II / III)							
Panzer Artillerie Regiment							
59	11	392	1,251 (77)	1,302	193	53	
(*) 6 x PzBefh III (+) 3 x SdKfz 250/2 / 5 x SdKfz 250/5 / 12 (+ 4 ammunition carriers) x SdKfz 124 / 6 (+3 amm. Carriers) SdKfz 165 (*) 12 x le FH 105mm / 8 x schw FH 150mm / 4 x 10cm Kanone							
Heeres Flak Artillerie Abteilung							
21	3	174	679 (47)	767	58	22	
(*) 4 x 20mm Flakvierling 38/1 SdKfz 7/1 (guns: 8 x 88mm Flak 36/37 / 24 x 20mm Flak 38 towed)							
Panzer Pionier Bataillon							
23	5	157	1,045 (74)	897	111	69 (6)	4
(+) 1 x SdKfz 251/1 / 2 x SdKfz 251/2 / 5 x SdKfz 251/3 / 23 x SdKfz 251/7 / 4 x SdKfz 251/10							
Panzer Division Nachrichten Abteilung							
13	3	103	396 (12)	444	51	13	
(*) 2 x PzBefh III (+) 10 x SdKfz 251/3 / 6 x SdKfz 251/11 / 2 x SdKfz 251/19							
Feldersatz Bataillon							
17	1	91	64 (14)	73	86	50 (12)	6 (2)
2 x Flammenwerfer							
Versorgungstruppen (with: Nachschub, Kraftfahr, Verwaltung, Sanitäts, Feldpost, Feldgendarmerie)							
56	28	371	1,787 (302)	1,957	18	76	

Note: the gun column only shows towed models, all others are included under AFVs.

		Vehicles				
PAK (Pzschrk)	Guns	Cars	Lorries	HTs	MCs	AFVs (tanks)
3 (3)		23	31	5	38	+ 4
		100	219	53	88	+ 16 (207)
9 (81)	2 x le.IG	91	190	26	101	+ 144
9 (81)		140	219	31	93	+ 25
3 (3)	2 x le.IG	32	73	6	91	+ 124
		38	74	26	21	+ 4 (45)
	* 24 9 x Flak 38	119	227	38	31	+ 33 (* 6)
	8 x Flak 88mm 24 x Flak 38	58	117	10	19	* 4
(6)		42	193	21	61	+ 35
		28	64	2	14	+ 18 (* 2)
1	1 x Flak 38 1 x le FH	7	2			
		93	537	8	105	

Table 2: 1944 Panzer Division

Personnel				Weapons			
Offs	Beamten	NCOs	ORs (Hiwi)	Rifles	MPs	LMG (HMG)	Mortars (heavy)
Divisions Kommando (with Divisions Kartenstelle and Begleit Kompanie)							
26	10	84	236 (17)	208	18	12 (2)	2
(*) 4 x SdKfz 10/4							
Panzer Regiment							
59	7	750	1,190 (72)	826	271	29	
(+) 6 x SdKfz 7/1 / 6 x SdKfz 251/7 / 4 x SdKfz 251/8							
(8 x Flakpanzer IV / 79 x Panther / 81 x PzKpfw IV / 2 x Bergepanzer III)							
Panzergrenadier Regiment (gepanzert, with 9–10. Kompanie)							
57	7	448	1,781 (64)	1,366	338	137 (23)	2 (8)
(+) 6 x SdKfz 138/1 / 41 x SdKfz 251/1 / 6 x SdKfz 251/2 / 19 x SdKfz 251/3 / 6 x SdKfz 251/7 / 1 x SdKfz 251/8 / 12 x SdKfz 251/9 / 7 x SdKfz 251/11 / 6 x SdKfz 251/16 / 22 x SdKfz 251/17							
Panzergrenadier Regiment (motorisiert, with 9–10. Kompanie)							
55	6	410	1,787 (60)	1,449	235	272 (52)	2 (8)
(+) 6 x SdKfz 138/1 / 3 x SdKfz 251/1 / 1 x SdKfz 251/3 / 1 x SdKfz 251/11							
Panzer Aufklärungs Abteilung							
24	3	221	701 (28)	447	204	46 (3)	
(+) 13 x SdKfz 234/1 / 3 x SdKfz 234/3 / 25 x SdKfz 250/1 / 9 x SdKfz 250/5 / 3 x SdKfz 250/7 / 2 x SdKfz 250/8 / 16 x SdKfz 250/9 / 12 x SdKfz 251/1 / 9 x SdKfz 251/2 / 13 x SdKfz 251/3 / 7 x SdKfz 251/7 / 1 x SdKfz 251/8 / 8 x SdKfz 251/9 / 3 x SdKfz 251/11 / 7 x SdKfz 251/17							
Panzerjäger Abteilung							
17	3	166	327 (21)	271	100	16	
(*) 1 x SdKfz 251/8 (31 x Panzerjäger IV / 2 x BergePanzer III)							
Panzer Artillerie Regiment							
56	11	349	1,038 (63)	1,107	155	40	
(*) 5 x PzBefh III/IV (+) 4 x SdKfz 250/5 / 12 (+4 ammunition carriers) x SdKfz 124 SP guns / 6 (+2 amm. Carriers) SdKfz 165 SP guns (*) 12 x le FH 105mm / 8 x schw FH 150mm / 4 x 10cm Kanone							
Heeres Flak Artillerie Abteilung							
18	3	125	443 (30)	509	42	12	
(*) 3 x 20mm Flakvierling 38/1 SdKfz 7/1 / 3 x 37mm Flak 43/1 SdKfz 7/2 (guns: 8 x 88mm Flak 36/37 / 6 x 20mm Flak 38 / 6 x 37mm Flak 43/1)							
Panzer Pionier Bataillon							
20	5	126	789 (32)	649	106	65 (6)	4
(+) 1 x SdKfz 251/1 / 2 x SdKfz 251/2 / 7 x SdKfz 251/3 / 18 x SdKfz 251/7 / 3 x SdKfz 251/17							
Panzer Division Nachrichten Abteilung							
13	4	101	358 (17)	379	53	12	
(*) 2 x PzBefh III/IV (+) 10 x SdKfz 251/3 / 4 x SdKfz 251/11 / 2 x SdKfz 251/19							
Feldersatz Bataillon (same as Panzer Division 43)							
Versorgungstruppen (with: Nachschub, Kraftfahr, Verwaltung, Sanitäts, Feldpost, Feldgendarmerie)							
49	25	348	1,624 (268)	1,819	29	77	

PAK (Pzschrk)	Guns	Vehicles Cars	Lorries	HTs	MCs	AFVs (tanks)
(3)		23	31	6	36	* 4
		70	192	48	41	+ 16 (170)
	6 x Flak 38	84	159	33	81	+ 126
	12 x Flak 38	124	199	44	83	+ 11
		18	55	8	22	+ 131
12		26	46	29	16	* 1 (33)
	* 24 9 x Flak 38	116	167	29	28	+ 28 (* 5)
	8 x Flak 88mm 6 x Flak 38 6 x Flak 43/1	30	69	14	12	* 6
(6)		27	95	24	42	+ 31
		33	61	2	14	+ 16 (* 2)
		90	458	26	75	

Table 3: late 1944 Panzer Division

Personnel				Weapons					Guns	Vehicles				AFVs
Offs	Beamten	NCOs	ORs (Hiwi)	Rifles	MPs	LMG (HMG)	Mortars (heavy)	PAK (Pzschrk)		Cars	Lorries	HTs	MCs	(tanks)
Divisions Kommando (same as earlier version of Panzer Division 1944)														
Panzer Regiment														
61	6	666	1,161 (44)	865	207	29		(18)		79	171	40	37	+ 16 (152)
(+) 6 x SdKfz 7/1 / 6 x SdKfz 251/7 / 4 x SdKfz 251/8 (8 x Flakpanzer IV / 67 x Panther / 69 x PzKpfw IV / 8 x Bergepanzer (IV / Panther))														
Panzergrenadier Regiment (gepanzert, with 9–10. Kompanie)														
58	4	386	1,537 (52)	1,181 (90)	342	117 (9)	(8)	(18)	6 x Flak 38	66	146	15	75	+ 126
(+) 6 x SdKfz 138/1 / 41 x SdKfz 251/1 / 6 x SdKfz 251/2 / 19 x SdKfz 251/3 / 6 x SdKfz 251/7 / 1 x SdKfz 251/8 / 12 x SdKfz 251/9 / 7 x SdKfz 251/16 / 22 x SdKfz 251/17														
Panzergrenadier Regiment (motorisiert, with 9–10. Kompanie)														
56	4	317	1,370 (53)	1,100 (180)	226	98	(8)	(33)	12 x Flak 38	74	178	25	74	+ 11
(+) 6 x SdKfz 138/1 / 3 x SdKfz 251/1 / 1 x SdKfz 251/3 / 1 x SdKfz 251/11														
Panzer Aufklärungs Abteilung														
25	2	229	694 (24)	564	214	45 (3)		(12)		25	50	4	20	+ 127
(+) 8 x SdKfz 234/1 / 7 x SdKfz 234/3 / 25 x SdKfz 250/1 / 9 x SdKfz 250/5 / 3 x SdKfz 250/7 / 2 x SdKfz 250/8 / 16 x SdKfz 250/9 / 12 x SdKfz 251/1 / 9 x SdKfz 251/2 / 11 x SdKfz 251/3 / 7 x SdKfz 251/7 / 1 x SdKfz 251/8 / 8 x SdKfz 251/9 / 2 x SdKfz 251/11 / 7 x SdKfz 251/17														
Panzerjäger Abteilung														
17	2	142	296 (15)	265	49	17		12 (6)		31	41	16	16	*1 (22)
(*) 1 x SdKfz 251/8 (21 x Panzerjäger IV / 38 / 1 x BergePanzer IV)														

The Panzer Artillerie Regiment, Heeres Flak Artillerie Abteilung, Panzer Pionier Bataillon, Panzer Division Nachrichten Abteilung, Feldersatz Bataillon, and Versorgungstruppen were all the same as the earlier version of the 1944 Panzer Division (see Table 2).

and 18 heavy mortars, 13 anti-tank guns plus 96 Panzerschreck, 25 field howitzers and guns, eight 88mm plus 36 20mm and six 37mm Flak guns, 601 cars, 1,469 lorries, 201 half-tracks, 529 motorcycles, 160 tanks (including eight Flakpanzer, 67 Panther, 69 PzKpfw IV and nine recovery), 21 Panzerjäger and 366 AFVs, including 16 self-propelled Flak, 36 guns of all types, about 300 armoured half-tracks (240 SdKfz 251, 59 SdKfz 250) and 15 armoured cars.

Divisional Headquarters

The Divisions Kommando, including the Staff (Stab), had at its disposal a mapping detachment (Divisions Kartenstelle) and, from early 1944, an escort company (Begleit Kompanie – KStN was issued on 1 February 1944) intended to provide protection but often also used as a reserve unit. Total strength of Divisions Kommando in 1943 included 22 officers, 10 Beamten (officials), 30 NCOs and 71 ORs, eight of which could be replaced by foreign auxiliaries (Hiwi). Vehicles included 15 cars, 15 lorries and eight motorcycles, and its armament comprised 86 rifles and three MPs. Revised KStN of 1 July 1944 increased overall strength of the Divisions Kommando (now with 23 officers, 51 NCOs, 76 ORs, 16 cars, 16 lorries, seven motorcycles, 83 rifles and four MPs), following the addition to the Stab of the Office of the National Socialist Officer (Nationalsozialistischer Führungs Offizier, NSFO).

The Begleit Kompanie was made up of a Panzergrenadier, a Panzerjäger, a Fla (light anti-aircraft) and an Erkunder (recce, later Kradschützen) Zug, and its total strength was three officers, 37 NCOs (later 32) and 179 ORs (later 153, of which nine could be Hiwi). Weapons included 135 (118 minus the Panzerjäger Zug) rifles, 19 (14) MPs, 15 (12) light and two heavy MGs, three Panzerschreck, two 81mm mortars, four self-propelled SdKfz 10/4 anti-aircraft 20mm guns and three anti-tank guns, which were eventually lost along with the entire Panzerjäger Zug following the new 1944 Panzer Division organization. Vehicles included eight (later seven) cars, 14 (13) lorries, five (six) half-tracked vehicles and 29 (28) motorcycles.

The Panzer Regiment

In 1943 the tank establishment of the Panzer Divisions existed on paper only, the exception being the attachment of available Panther-equipped Abteilungen to other divisions. The Panzer Regiment included a regimental Stab and a Stabs Kompanie with a Nachrichten (equipped with three Panther tanks) and an Aufklärungs Zug (equipped with five PzKpfw IV), plus a first Panther-equipped Panzer Abteilung and a second one equipped with PzKpfw IV. The former was made up of a Stab and a Stabs Kompanie (with a Nachrichten, Aufklärungs,

The regimental Panzer Werkstatt Kompanie always played a significant role in keeping the Panzers operational and in recovering damaged or faulty vehicles. Its 1 April 1944 establishment included 230 men, seven cars, 45 lorries and six motorcycles plus 14 half-tracked vehicles, mostly SdKfz 7 and 9 heavy tractors and their variants.

Panzer Regiment, 1 November 1943 establishment

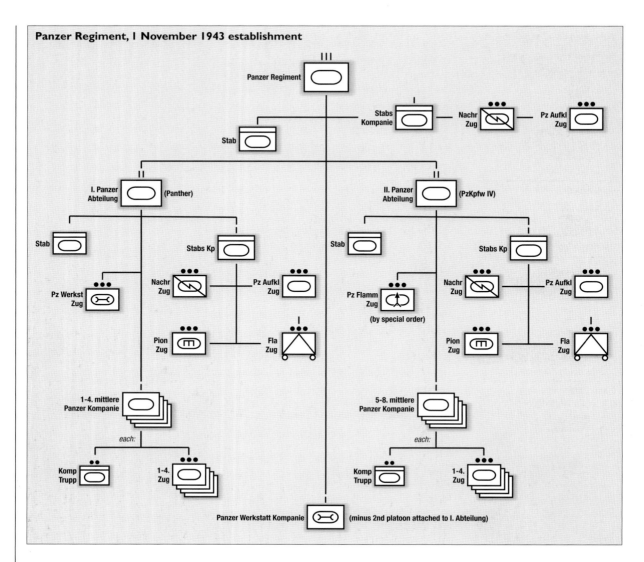

Pionier and Fla Zug) plus four Panther Kompanien and a Werkstatt Zug; overall strength was 26 officers, five Beamten, 422 NCOs and 708 ORs (63 Hiwi), armed with 502 rifles, 137 MPs and 22 light MGs (excluding vehicle-carried weapons) and equipped with 54 cars, 110 lorries, 29 half-tracked vehicles and 34 motorcycles. The establishment indicated 96 Panther tanks, but one Panzer Zug from each Kompanie was often missing (to be formed only if tanks were available, a rarity with the Panther) thus shrinking overall strength to a grand total of 76 tanks. The PzKpfw IV-equipped Panzer Abteilung had a similar organization to the Panther Abteilung, the only differences being the possible availability of a Panzer Flamm Zug, and the fact that it had Werkstatt Kompanie detached from the regiment minus the second Zug, to the Panther Abteilung. Overall strength was 29 officers, four Beamten, 402 NCOs and 689 ORs (45 Hiwi), armed with 451 rifles, 148 MPs and 24 light MGs and with 41 cars, 96 lorries, 28 half-tracked vehicles and 44 motorcycles. Tank strength was 93 PzKpfw IV plus up to 10 PzKpfw III of various kinds; however, not only were the latter either missing (Flamm Zug) or eventually replaced by PzKpfw IV tanks in the Stabskompanie, but also one platoon could again be missing from each company. Therefore, the overall tank strength of a 1943 Panzer Division varied from 160 (81 PzKpfw IV and 79 Panther) up to 200 (101 PzKpfw IV and 99 Panther) tanks.

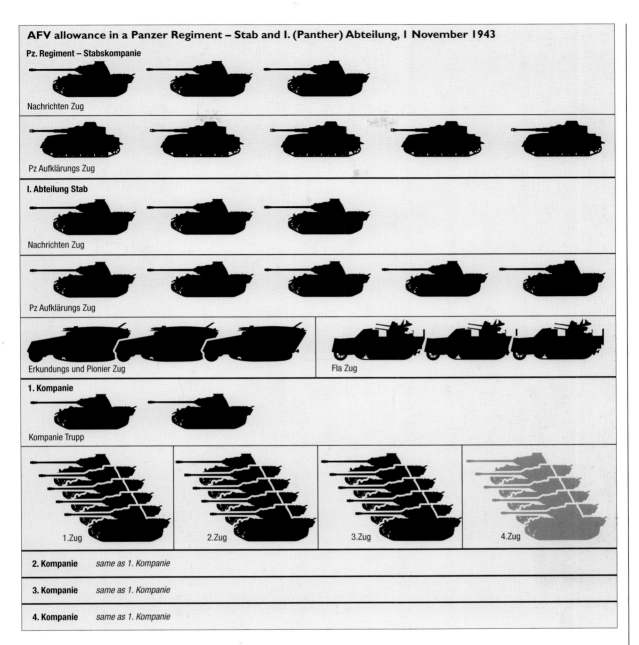

AFV allowance in a Panzer Regiment – Stab and I. (Panther) Abteilung, 1 November 1943

Pz. Regiment – Stabskompanie

Nachrichten Zug

Pz Aufklärungs Zug

I. Abteilung Stab

Nachrichten Zug

Pz Aufklärungs Zug

Erkundungs und Pionier Zug

Fla Zug

1. Kompanie

Kompanie Trupp

1.Zug

2.Zug

3.Zug

4.Zug

2. Kompanie   *same as 1. Kompanie*

3. Kompanie   *same as 1. Kompanie*

4. Kompanie   *same as 1. Kompanie*

The 1944 Panzer Division organization brought changes mainly at platoon level; a Panzer Fla Zug was added to the regimental Stab (it was to be equipped with the new Flakpanzer IV but, due to unavailability, Flakpanzer 38 were used instead) while, at battalion level, the Aufklärungs and Nachrichten Zug were merged together. Most important of all, the new organization of the Panzer Kompanien (now sharing the same KStN regardless of the type of tank equipping them) sanctioned the reduction from four to three Züge per company and therefore the drop from the official figure of 22 to the more realistic one of 17 tanks per company, with the result that every Panzer Abteilung now had only 76 tanks with a total of 79 Panther and 81 PzKpfw IV in the regiment. The overall strength was 15 to 30 per cent less in comparison with the 1943 organization (see tables 1 and 2), though the widespread lack of tanks eventually brought about a further reduction in the amended KStN of

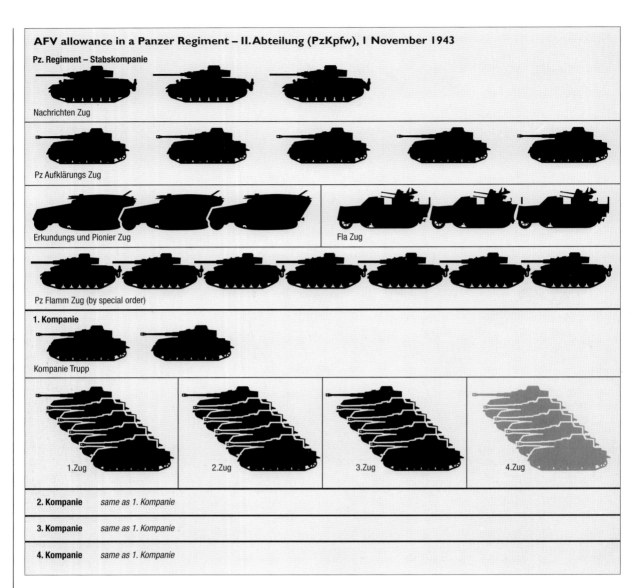

AFV allowance in a Panzer Regiment – II. Abteilung (PzKpfw), 1 November 1943

Pz. Regiment – Stabskompanie

Nachrichten Zug

Pz Aufklärungs Zug

Erkundungs und Pionier Zug

Fla Zug

Pz Flamm Zug (by special order)

1. Kompanie

Kompanie Trupp

1.Zug

2.Zug

3.Zug

4.Zug

2. Kompanie	*same as 1. Kompanie*
3. Kompanie	*same as 1. Kompanie*
4. Kompanie	*same as 1. Kompanie*

The Ausf D was the last variant of the SdKfz 251 armoured half-track; over 10,000 were built from 1943 onwards. Only slightly longer than the Ausf C variant, it retained all of the latter's characteristics. Due to its increasing availability, in late 1943 the SdKfz 251 equipped at least one Panzergrenadier Bataillon per division.

Panzer Regiment, 1 April 1944 establishment

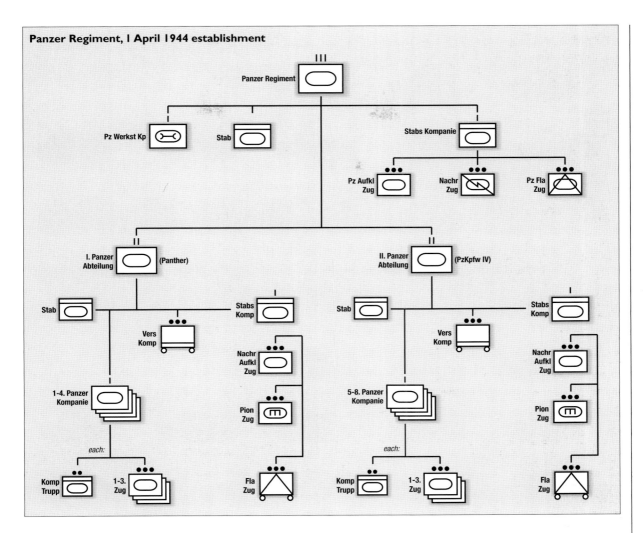

1 November 1944 which, although it brought with it few major changes to organization, greatly influenced equipment availability. The new KStN for the Panzer Kompanie in fact sanctioned the concept of a mixed Panzer Abteilung, with every company now equipped either with the Panther, the PzKpfw IV or the Jagdpanzer IV/70 (if not the Sturmgeschütz) tanks and tank hunters. Moreover, every Panzer Kompanie could have either the customary 17 tanks or the more realistic figure of 14, with a single tank dropped from every Zug. The grand total shrank to 136 tanks, Bergepanzers excluded, though regimental strength did not drop dramatically and in some cases even increased in comparison with the earlier organization (see Table 3).

A few words must be devoted to the assault gun, the Sturmgeschütz, which, without being officially part of the organization, was otherwise widely used in the Panzer Divisions especially between 1943 and early 1944, when making good for the lack of the Panther Abteilung. Provisions were made for the creation of the Panzer Sturmgeschütz Abteilung, with an organization similar to that of the Panzer Abteilung in which Sturmgeschütze replaced tanks; however, since only three were actually formed, more often than not a Sturmgeschütz Brigade (actually a battalion) would be attached to a Panzer Division serving either as its Panzer or Panzerjäger Abteilung. According to the 1 June 1944 establishment a Sturmgeschütz Brigade had either 31 or 50 assault guns, making them more a stopgap expedient than a real solution.

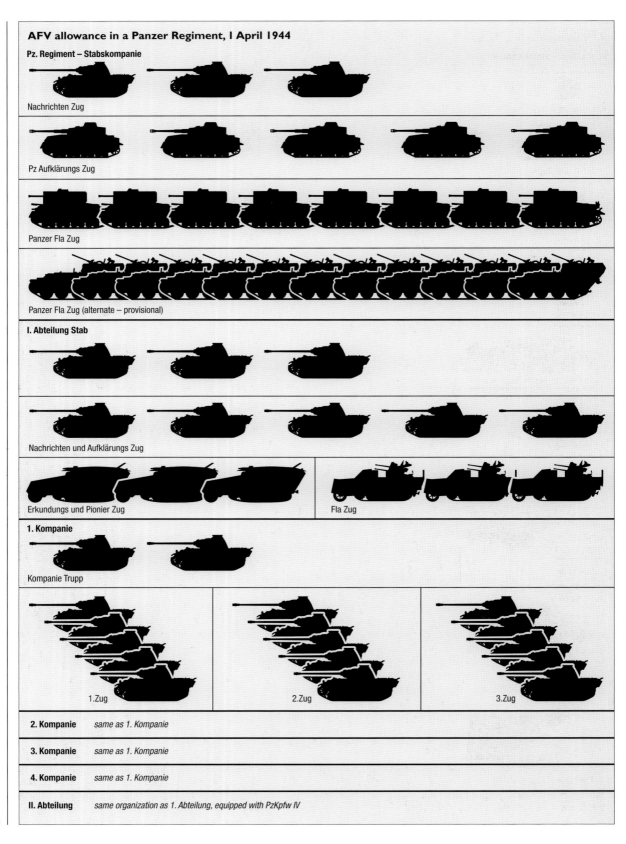

AFV allowance in a Panzer Regiment, 1 April 1944

Pz. Regiment – Stabskompanie

Nachrichten Zug

Pz Aufklärungs Zug

Panzer Fla Zug

Panzer Fla Zug (alternate – provisional)

I. Abteilung Stab

Nachrichten und Aufklärungs Zug

Erkundungs und Pionier Zug

Fla Zug

1. Kompanie

Kompanie Trupp

1.Zug

2.Zug

3.Zug

2. Kompanie	*same as 1. Kompanie*
3. Kompanie	*same as 1. Kompanie*
4. Kompanie	*same as 1. Kompanie*
II. Abteilung	*same organization as 1. Abteilung, equipped with PzKpfw IV*

AFV allowance in a Panzer Regiment (mixed), 1 November 1944

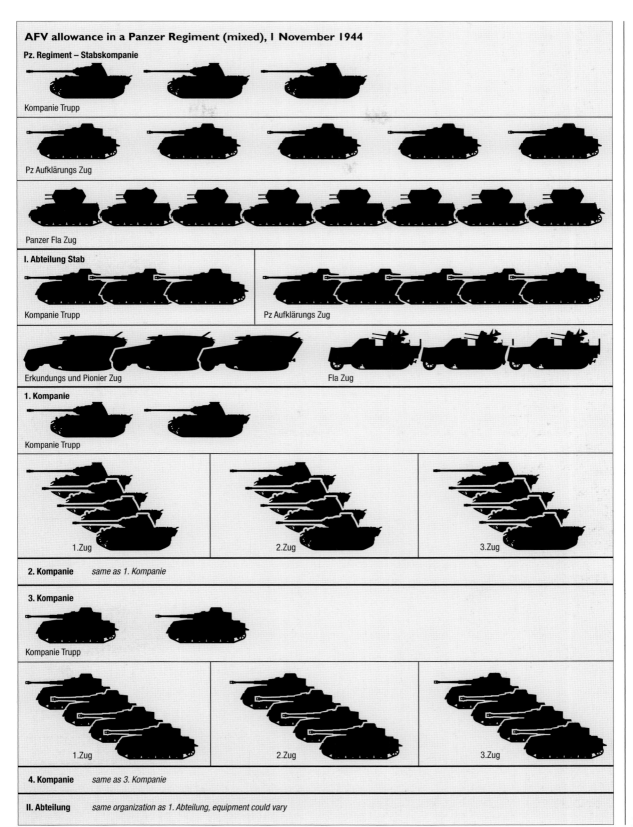

Pz. Regiment – Stabskompanie

Kompanie Trupp

Pz Aufklärungs Zug

Panzer Fla Zug

I. Abteilung Stab

Kompanie Trupp

Pz Aufklärungs Zug

Erkundungs und Pionier Zug

Fla Zug

1. Kompanie

Kompanie Trupp

1.Zug

2.Zug

3.Zug

2. Kompanie   *same as 1. Kompanie*

3. Kompanie

Kompanie Trupp

1.Zug

2.Zug

3.Zug

4. Kompanie   *same as 3. Kompanie*

II. Abteilung   *same organization as 1. Abteilung, equipment could vary*

Panzergrenadier units

In spite of the worsening situation, in 1943–44 Panzergrenadier units were better armed, motorized and equipped than ever before. According to the 1943 Panzer Division establishment, an armoured infantry regiment (Panzergrenadier Regiment gepanzert) included a Stab and Stabskompanie with a Kradschützen (recce), a Flammenwerfer, a Panzerjäger and a Nachrichten Zug, two Panzergrenadier Bataillone – one of which was mounted on Schützen Panzer Wagen APCs (the old designation was still used even after the introduction of the new one – Mannschaft Transport Wagen – when Schützen units were renamed Panzergrenadiers in July 1942) – plus one regimental Fla Kompanie (only to be formed if equipment was available), one schwere Infanterie Geschütz (heavy infantry gun, with six armoured self-propelled SdKfz 138/1) and one Panzergrenadier Pionier Kompanie, which included two motorized and one armoured Zug plus one Granatenwerfer and one schwere MG Gruppe. This was particularly strong with four officers, 30 NCOs, 184 ORs (eight of which could be replaced by Hiwi), 141 rifles, 30 MPs, 14 light and two heavy MGs, three Panzerschreck, two 81mm mortars and three cars, 25 lorries, six motorcycles and eight SdKfz 251 APCs (one command SdKfz 251/3, six engineer SdKfz 251/7, one gun-armed SdKfz 251/10).

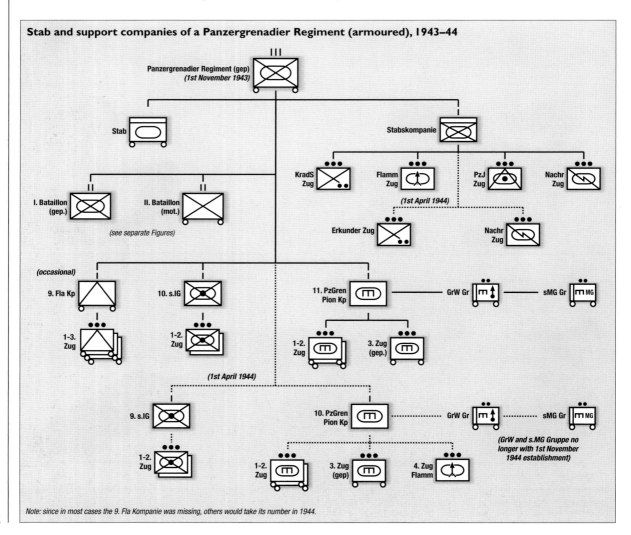

Stab and support companies of a Panzergrenadier Regiment (armoured), 1943–44

Note: since in most cases the 9. Fla Kompanie was missing, others would take its number in 1944.

Both Panzergrenadier battalions had considerable strength; in November 1943 a Panzergrenadier Bataillon (gepanzert) included three armoured companies plus a schwere Kompanie with two gun and one Panzerjäger platoons. A single Panzergrenadier Kompanie had three Züge and a fourth schwere Zug, the latter including two schwere MG Gruppen, a Granatenwerfer and a Kanonen Gruppe, and its strength was three officers, 52 NCOs, 165 ORs (three Hiwi), 122 rifles, 55 MPs, 18 light and four heavy MGs, three Panzerschreck, two cars, six lorries, one non-armoured half-track and six motorcycles, plus 22 SdKfz 251 armoured half-tracks (two command SdKfz 251/3, nine APCs SdKfz 251/1, two mortar-carrier SdKfz 251/2, two 75mm gun-carrier SdKfz 251/9, seven 37mm gun-armed SdKfz 251/10). It is worth noting that there was excessive optimism about the availability of new vehicles since the original KStN included six 20mm gun-armed SdKfz 251/17 (in the schwere Kompanie they were also used as tractors for anti-tank guns) which, still undergoing development, were actually replaced with the 37mm gun-armed SdKfz 251/10. The total strength of the schwere Kompanie was four officers, 32 NCOs, 100 ORs (4 Hiwi), 83 rifles, 34 MPs, three light MGs, two light 75mm infantry guns, three 75mm Panzer Abwehr Kanonen (PAK) two cars, eight lorries, one non-armoured half-track and seven motorcycles plus 19 SdKfz 251. The total strength of the Panzergrenadier Bataillon was 21 officers, three Beamten, 216 NCOs, 688 ORs (26 Hiwi), 552 rifles, 208 MPs (including those

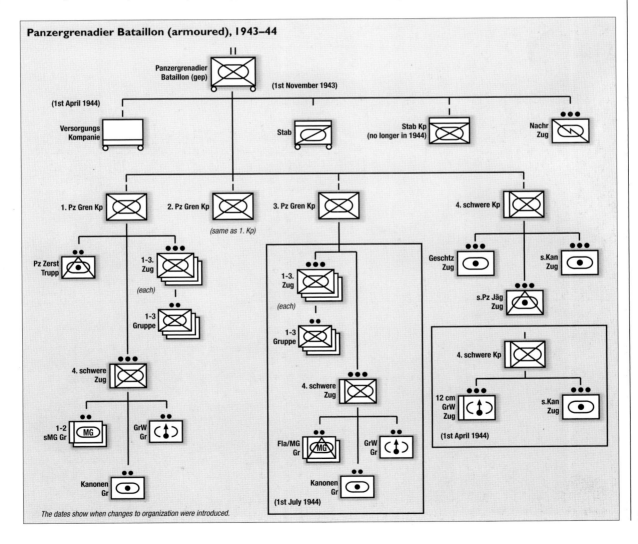

Panzergrenadier Bataillon (armoured), 1943–44

The dates show when changes to organization were introduced.

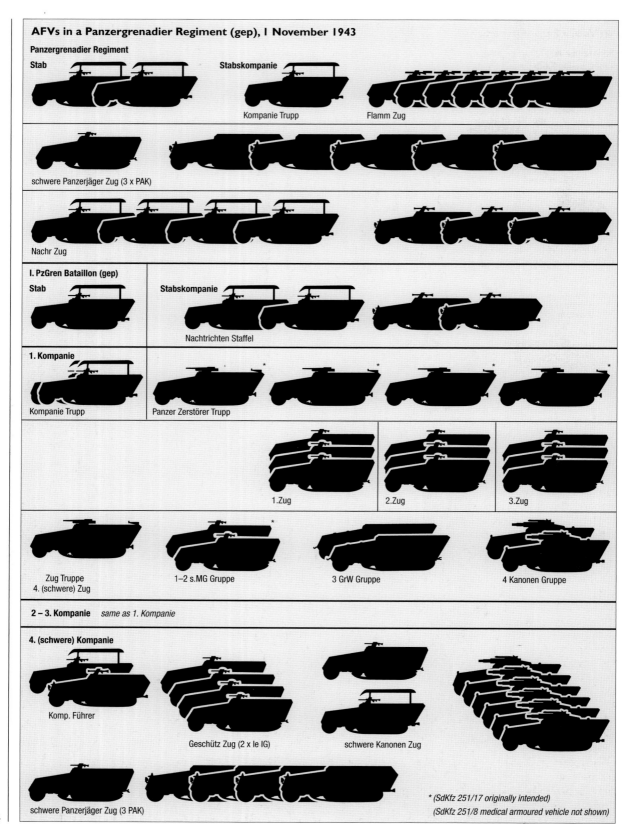

AFVs in a Panzergrenadier Regiment (gep), 1 November 1943

Panzergrenadier Regiment

Stab

Stabskompanie

Kompanie Trupp

Flamm Zug

schwere Panzerjäger Zug (3 x PAK)

Nachr Zug

I. PzGren Bataillon (gep)

Stab

Stabskompanie

Nachrichten Staffel

1. Kompanie

Kompanie Trupp

Panzer Zerstörer Trupp

1.Zug

2.Zug

3.Zug

Zug Truppe
4. (schwere) Zug

1–2 s.MG Gruppe

3 GrW Gruppe

4 Kanonen Gruppe

2 – 3. Kompanie *same as 1. Kompanie*

4. (schwere) Kompanie

Komp. Führer

Geschütz Zug (2 x le IG)

schwere Kanonen Zug

schwere Panzerjäger Zug (3 PAK)

* (SdKfz 251/17 originally intended)

(SdKfz 251/8 medical armoured vehicle not shown)

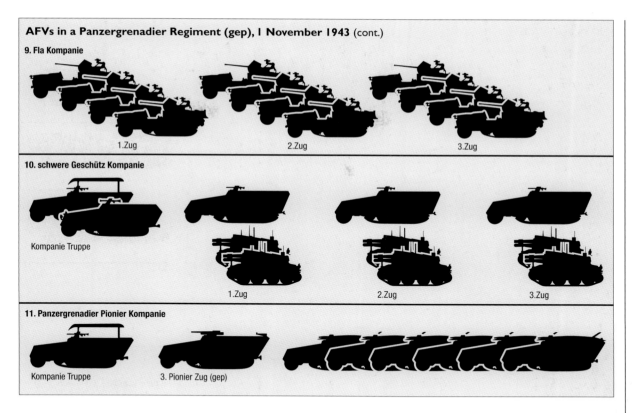

AFVs in a Panzergrenadier Regiment (gep), I November 1943 (cont.)

9. Fla Kompanie

1.Zug 2.Zug 3.Zug

10. schwere Geschütz Kompanie

Kompanie Truppe

1.Zug 2.Zug 3.Zug

11. Panzergrenadier Pionier Kompanie

Kompanie Truppe 3. Pionier Zug (gep)

aboard the AFVs), 57 light and 12 heavy MGs (excluding AFVs mounted ones), 39 Panzerschreck, two leichte IG, three PAK, 16 cars, 44 lorries, six non-armoured and 91 armoured half-tracks and 30 motorcycles. The Panzergrenadier Bataillon (motorisiert), though stronger, was less mobile and had reduced firepower; it had 19 officers, three Beamten, 176 NCOs, 705 ORs (31 Hiwi), 579 rifles, 96 MPs, 59 light and 21 heavy MGs, 39 Panzerschreck, three PAK, six 81mm and four 120mm mortars, 52 cars, 81 lorries, nine half-tracks and 24 motorcycles.

The striking differences between armoured and motorized Panzergrenadier Bataillone eventually supplied the Panzer Divisions with two quite different infantry units, with the armoured Panzergrenadier Regiment being stronger and also better suited to keeping up with the Panzer Regiment. This would not last for long, however, since the new 1944 Panzer Division organization brought some changes to both organization and strength. First of all every schwere Zug of the Panzergrenadier Kompanie lost one heavy MG Gruppe, the remaining one being replaced by a Fla und MG Gruppe (anti-aircraft and MG section, now equipped with the SdKfz 251/17); also, the schwere Kompanie was now down to the heavy Granatenwerfer and Kanonen Zug. Total strength of the Panzergrenadier Kompanie shrank to three officers, 36 NCOs, 151 ORs, 94 rifles, 44 MPs, 18 light MGs, two cars, four motorcycles and a total of 23 SdKfz 251 of various kinds, the gepanzertes Panzergrenadier Bataillon having now 21 officers, three Beamten, 172 NCOs, 645 ORs (23 Hiwi), 444 rifles, 173 MPS, 58 light and nine heavy MGs, four 120mm mortars, 17 cars, 30 lorries, 24 motorcycles and six non-armoured plus 101 armoured half-tracks. Worst of all, a lack of weapons, vehicles and equipment greatly hampered the reorganization of those gepanzert Panzergrenadier units, and the creation of any new ones. Given also a widespread lack of motor vehicles, on 1 November 1944 a new organization was developed which not only reduced overall strength, but also envisaged the creation of the new bicycle-mounted (Fahrrad bewegliche) Panzergrenadier Kompanie which, though desperately lacking

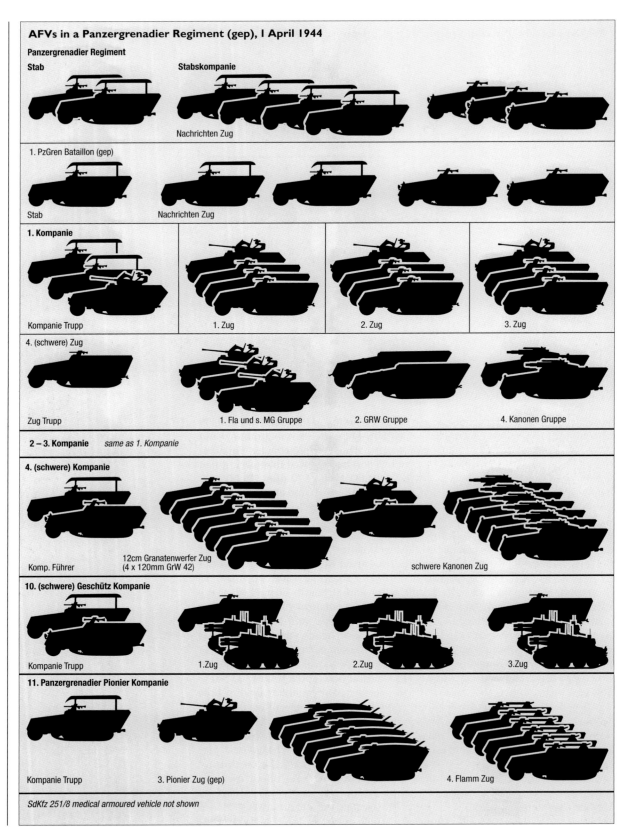

AFVs in a Panzergrenadier Regiment (gep), 1 April 1944

Panzergrenadier Regiment

Stab   Stabskompanie

Nachrichten Zug

1. PzGren Bataillon (gep)

Stab   Nachrichten Zug

1. Kompanie

Kompanie Trupp   1. Zug   2. Zug   3. Zug

4. (schwere) Zug

Zug Trupp   1. Fla und s. MG Gruppe   2. GRW Gruppe   4. Kanonen Gruppe

2 – 3. Kompanie   *same as 1. Kompanie*

4. (schwere) Kompanie

Komp. Führer   12cm Granatenwerfer Zug
(4 x 120mm GrW 42)   schwere Kanonen Zug

10. (schwere) Geschütz Kompanie

Kompanie Trupp   1.Zug   2.Zug   3.Zug

11. Panzergrenadier Pionier Kompanie

Kompanie Trupp   3. Pionier Zug (gep)   4. Flamm Zug

SdKfz 251/8 medical armoured vehicle not shown

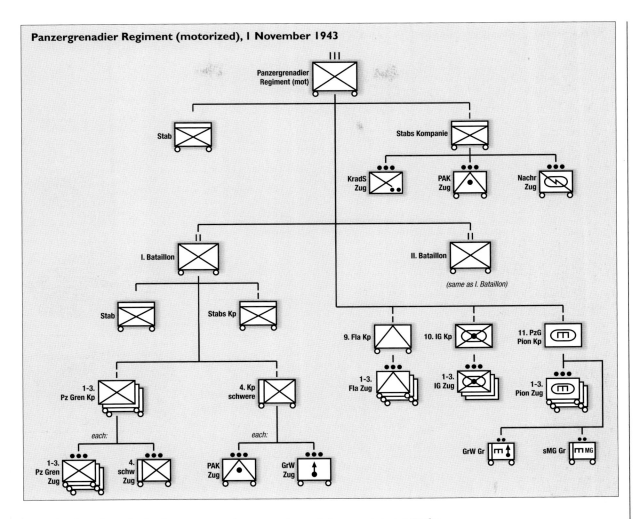

Panzergrenadier Regiment (motorized), 1 November 1943

motorization (it only had one car and one motorcycle) was comparatively better armed since its first Zug was now turned into a Sturm Zug completely armed with the Sturmgewehr 44, the new assault rifle. Its strength was three officers, 17 NCOs, 120 ORs and it had 67 rifles plus 37 Sturmgewehre, 15 MPs, 12 light MGs and three Panzerschreck.

Though lacking the mobility and firepower of the armoured version, the Panzergrenadier Regiment (motorisiert) was a more common occurrence and also a kind of unit which would better suit the Panzer Divisions' tactical needs when fighting in defence. Though overall organization matched that of its armoured parent, the schwere Kompanie of its Panzergrenadier Bataillon only had one Panzerjäger and one Granatenwerfer Zug with a total of three officers, 22 NCOs, 90 ORs (seven Hiwi), 84 rifles, 13 MPs, five light MGs, three 75mm PAK, four 120mm heavy mortars, six cars, eight lorries, eight half-tracks and four motorcycles. The motorized Panzergrenadier Kompanie included a Panzerzerstörer Trupp (tank destroyer section), three Züge and a schwere Zug with two schwere MG Gruppen and a Granatenwerfer Gruppe for a total of three officers, 44 NCOs, 178 ORs (three Hiwi), 134 rifles, 27 MPs, 18 light and four heavy MGs, 13 Panzerschreck, two 81mm mortars, 12 cars, 18 lorries and five motorcycles. In any case, the Panzergrenadier Regiment (motorisiert) had the same Fla and IG Kompanie as the gepanzert version, while its Panzergrenadier Pionier Kompanie was motorized (it had three officers, 33 NCOs, 182 ORs with eight Hiwi, 152 rifles, 24 MPs, 12 light and four heavy MGs, three Panzerschreck,

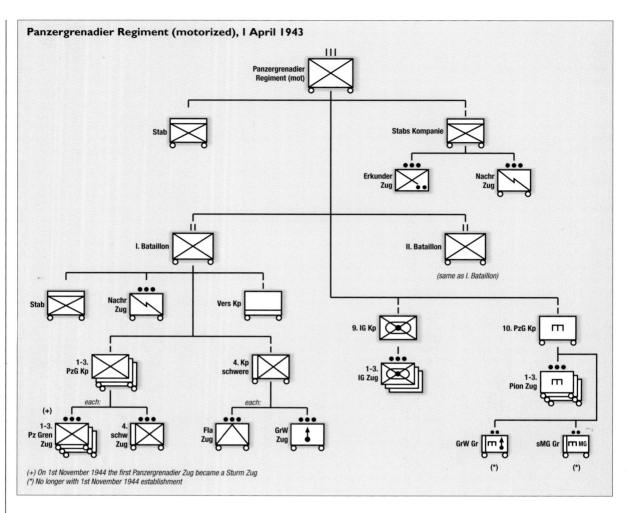

Panzergrenadier Regiment (motorized), 1 April 1943

III — Panzergrenadier Regiment (mot)

Stab

Stabs Kompanie
- Erkunder Zug
- Nachr Zug

II — I. Bataillon
II — II. Bataillon *(same as I. Bataillon)*

I. Bataillon:
- Stab
- Nachr Zug
- Vers Kp
- 1-3. PzG Kp *(+)*
  - each:
    - 1-3. Pz Gren Zug
    - 4. schw Zug
- 4. Kp schwere
  - each:
    - Fla Zug
    - GrW Zug

II. Bataillon:
- 9. IG Kp
  - 1-3. IG Zug
- 10. PzG Kp
  - 1-3. Pion Zug
    - GrW Gr *(*)*
    - sMG Gr *(*)*

(+) On 1st November 1944 the first Panzergrenadier Zug became a Sturm Zug
(*) No longer with 1st November 1944 establishment

two 81mm mortars, seven cars, 28 lorries and seven motorcycles). Losses and overall lack of weapons, equipment and vehicles also affected the organization of the motorized Panzergrenadier Bataillon; the 1944 Panzer Division organization brought about, in the same manner as the armoured one, the disappearance of PAK units (the PAK Zug in the schwere Kompanie were replaced by a Fla one) and to the creation of the Versorgungs Kompanie, plus an overall reduction in strength. The Panzergrenadier Kompanie now had three officers, 29 NCOs, 165

The SdKfz 162/1 Jagdpanzer IV/70, which entered production in August 1944, was built on the chassis of the SdKfz 162 Jagdpanzer IV (which it was intended to replace) with a few modifications, most notably the more powerful 75 mm L/70 gun. Note the Panzergrenadier carrying two different models of the Panzerfaust.

ORs, 115 rifles, 23 MPs, 18 light and four heavy MGs, 11 cars, 13 lorries and four motorcycles; the schwere Kompanie had three officers, 22 NCOs, 79 ORs, 63 rifles, 17 MPs, two light MGs, six towed 20mm Flak 38, four 120mm heavy mortars, five cars, three lorries, 11 tracked or half-tracked vehicles and five motorcycles. The new organization of 1 November 1944 brought further changes including the introduction of one Sturm Zug in every Panzergrenadier Kompanie, which now had three officers, 18 NCOs, 105 ORs, 60 rifles plus 30 Sturmgewehre, 21 MPs, 12 light MGs, three Panzerschreck, one car, eight lorries and three motorcycles (the schwere Kompanie now had three officers, 21 NCOs, 79 ORs, 62 rifles, 16 MPs, two light MGs its heavy weapons and vehicles allowance unchanged). As a consequence, overall strength of the motorized Panzergrenadier Bataillon changed between 1 April and 1 November from 20 to 21 officers, three to two Beamten, 148 to 117 NCOs, 697 to 506 ORs (23 to 21 Hiwi), 548 to 382 rifles (plus 90 Sturmgewehre in November), 91 to 86 MPs, 60 to 41 light MGs, 12 to none heavy MGs, none to 12 Panzerschreck, 50 to 24 cars, 75 to 62 lorries, 17 to 12 tracked or half-tracked vehicles, 25 to 21 motorcycles (the allowance of six towed 20mm Flak 38 and four heavy 120mm mortars was unchanged). In one year, the overall strength of the Panzergrenadier Regiment (motorisiert) had dropped from 2,513 all ranks in November 1943 to 2,258 in April and eventually to 1,747 in November 1944 (see tables 1 to 3), which clearly influenced the fighting power of the Panzer Division.

Panzeraufklärungs Abteilung

The development of armoured reconnaissance units in 1943–44 reflected their growing role as combat units, leaving reconnaissance duties mainly to Panzerspäh (armoured car) units. Yet, in spite of their designation, more often than not the Panzerspäh units would have been equipped with the light SdKfz

The last variant of the Sturmgeschütz III, the Ausf G, was produced from early 1943 and became the most widely diffused. The modified cast gun mantlet, known as the 'Saukopf' (boar's head), was introduced in the latest production batches while a Zimmerit (anti-magnetic paste) coating became common in late 1943.

An SdKfz 233 armoured car armed with a 75mm L/24 gun, the same one that once equipped the early PzKpfw IV. 109 examples were produced between December 1942 and October 1943, which were used to equip the schwere Panzerspäh Zug of the Panzer Aufklärungs Abteilung until replaced by the gun-armed SdKfz 251/9.

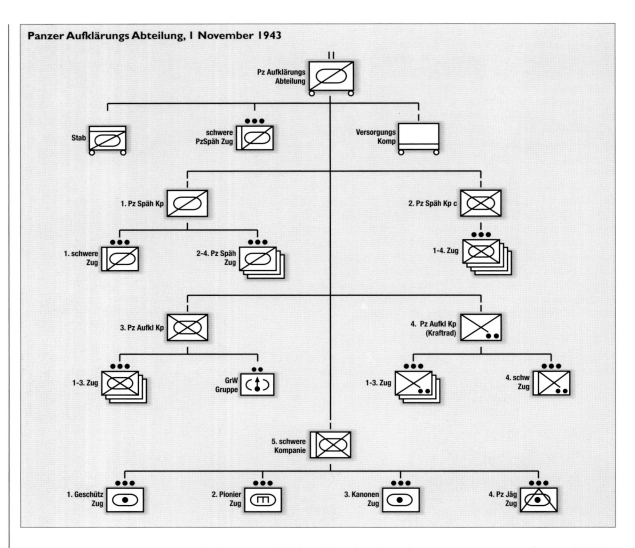

Panzer Aufklärungs Abteilung, 1 November 1943

Pz Aufklärungs Abteilung

Stab

schwere PzSpäh Zug

Versorgungs Komp

1. Pz Späh Kp

2. Pz Späh Kp c

1. schwere Zug

2-4. Pz Späh Zug

1-4. Zug

3. Pz Aufkl Kp

4. Pz Aufkl Kp (Kraftrad)

1-3. Zug

GrW Gruppe

1-3. Zug

4. schw Zug

5. schwere Kompanie

1. Geschütz Zug

2. Pionier Zug

3. Kanonen Zug

4. Pz Jäg Zug

250 armoured half-tracks rather than the customary armoured cars which, in the last years of war, became scarce. In November 1943 the organization of the Panzeraufklärungs Abteilung had not changed from earlier in the same year; it included a Stab, a schwere Panzerspäh Zug (formed according to availability), a first Panzerspäh Kompanie (with one heavy and three light Züge), a second Panzerspäh Kompanie c (four Züge, all equipped with SdKfz 250), a third half-track mounted Panzeraufklärung Kompanie (three Züge plus a Granatenwerfer Gruppe) and a motorcycle-mounted Panzeraufklärung Kompanie (three plus a heavy Zug), which could be replaced by a similar one equipped either with Kettenkrad (the semi-tracked motorcycle) or with Volkswagen cars. It was intended to be equipped later on like the third company. Also there were a schwere Kompanie (with two gun, one engineer and one anti-tank platoons) and a Versorgungs Kompanie.

Several changes were introduced with the 1944 Panzer Division organization; all Panzerspäh units still equipped with armoured cars were incorporated in the Stabskompanie forming one Geschütz and two schwere Panzerspäh Züge, while Panzerspäh Kompanie c became the first company. Also, the third Panzeraufklärungs Kompanie was reorganized as a second leichte Panzeraufklärungs Kompanie and the organization of the fourth Panzeraufklärungs Kompanie was now the same as the Panzergrenadier

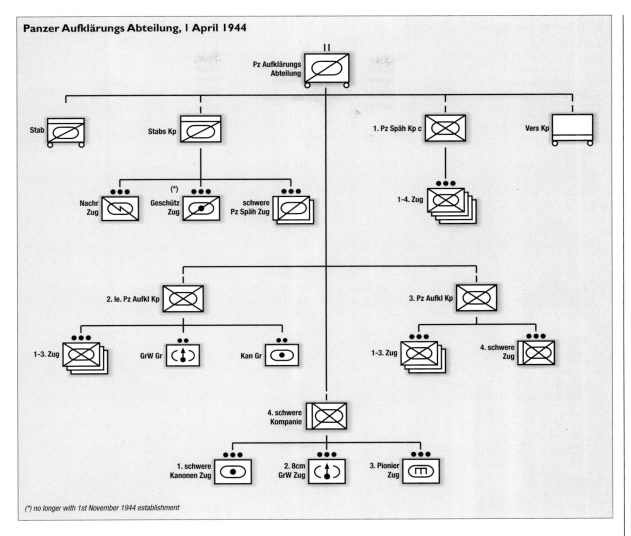

Panzer Aufklärungs Abteilung, 1 April 1944

- Pz Aufklärungs Abteilung
- Stab
- Stabs Kp
  - Nachr Zug
  - (*) Geschütz Zug
  - schwere Pz Späh Zug
- 1. Pz Späh Kp c
  - 1-4. Zug
- Vers Kp
- 2. le. Pz Aufkl Kp
  - 1-3. Zug
  - GrW Gr
  - Kan Gr
- 3. Pz Aufkl Kp
  - 1-3. Zug
  - 4. schwere Zug
- 4. schwere Kompanie
  - 1. schwere Kanonen Zug
  - 2. 8cm GrW Zug
  - 3. Pionier Zug

(*) no longer with 1st November 1944 establishment

company from a Panzergrenadier Bataillon (gep). The fourth schwere Kompanie lost the Geschütz Zug, replaced by a Granatenwerfer Zug, and the PAK Zug, which was not replaced. The overall strength changed between November 1943 and November 1944, shrinking from 1,073 to 949 before eventually rising again to 950; on the other hand, vehicle allowances did not suffer. The number and quality of the available Panzerspäh increased, with the 12 eight-wheeled armoured cars of 1943 (six gun-armed SdKfz 233, three SdKfz 231 and three command SdKfz 232) being replaced by 13 new SdKfz 234/1 and three gun-armed SdKfz 234/3. Also, the organization of the Panzerspäh Kompanie c was practically unchanged (vehicle allowance was always the same and it always had three officers, switching from 59 NCOs and 49 ORs in November 1943 to 29 and 28 NCOs and 53 ORs in April and November 1944), like that of the Panzeraufklärungs Kompanie (always three officers, 45 to 39 and 38 NCOs between November 1943 and November 1944 and 149 to 125 ORs), which lost only one mortar and one gun-armed SdKfz 250/7 and /8 and increased from 24 (21 SdKfz 250/1 plus three /3) to 25 (all SdKfz 250/1) the number of its APCs. In addition, changes brought to the schwere Kompanie did not affect the overall fighting power of the Panzeraufklärungs Abteilung, which was increased by the addition of the Panzergrenadier/Panzeraufklärungs Kompanie.

AFVs in a Panzer Aufklärungs Abteilung, 1 November 1943

Panzer Aufklärungs Abteilung
Stab

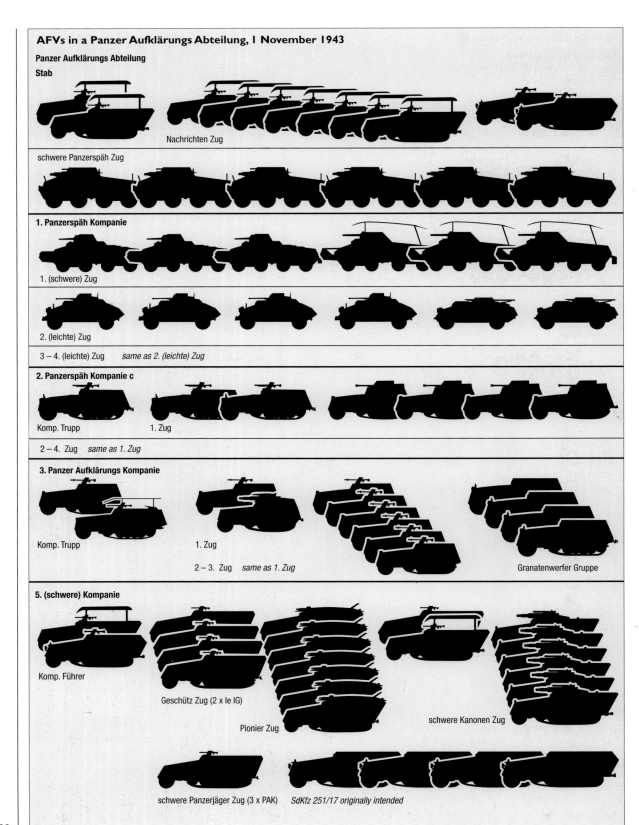

Nachrichten Zug

schwere Panzerspäh Zug

1. Panzerspäh Kompanie

1. (schwere) Zug

2. (leichte) Zug

3 – 4. (leichte) Zug   *same as 2. (leichte) Zug*

2. Panzerspäh Kompanie c

Komp. Trupp   1. Zug

2 – 4. Zug   *same as 1. Zug*

3. Panzer Aufklärungs Kompanie

Komp. Trupp

1. Zug

2 – 3. Zug   *same as 1. Zug*   Granatenwerfer Gruppe

5. (schwere) Kompanie

Komp. Führer

Geschütz Zug (2 x le IG)

Pionier Zug

schwere Kanonen Zug

schwere Panzerjäger Zug (3 x PAK)   *SdKfz 251/17 originally intended*

AFVs in a Panzer Aufklärungs Abteilung, 1 April 1944

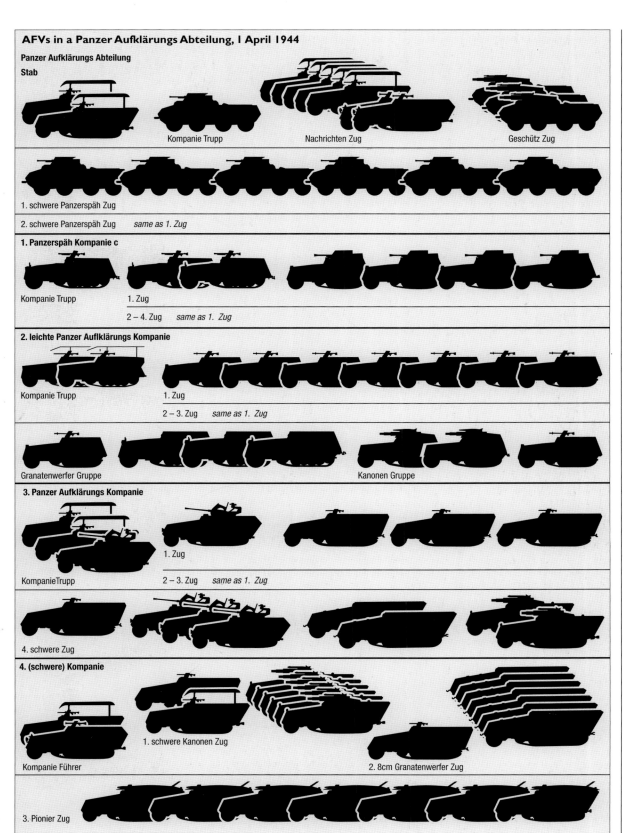

Panzer Aufklärungs Abteilung

Stab

Kompanie Trupp   Nachrichten Zug   Geschütz Zug

1. schwere Panzerspäh Zug

2. schwere Panzerspäh Zug   *same as 1. Zug*

1. Panzerspäh Kompanie c

Kompanie Trupp   1. Zug

2 – 4. Zug   *same as 1. Zug*

2. leichte Panzer Auflklärungs Kompanie

Kompanie Trupp   1. Zug

2 – 3. Zug   *same as 1. Zug*

Granatenwerfer Gruppe   Kanonen Gruppe

3. Panzer Aufklärungs Kompanie

1. Zug

KompanieTrupp   2 – 3. Zug   *same as 1. Zug*

4. schwere Zug

4. (schwere) Kompanie

Kompanie Führer   1. schwere Kanonen Zug   2. 8cm Granatenwerfer Zug

3. Pionier Zug

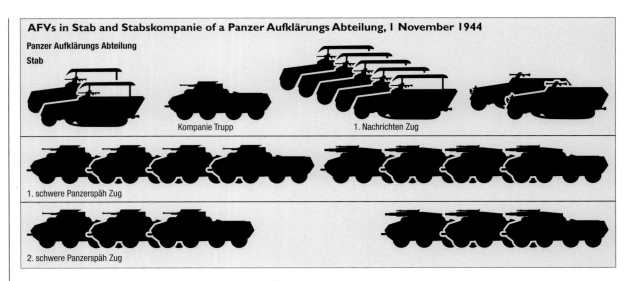

AFVs in Stab and Stabskompanie of a Panzer Aufklärungs Abteilung, 1 November 1944

Panzer Aufklärungs Abteilung
Stab

Kompanie Trupp

1. Nachrichten Zug

1. schwere Panzerspäh Zug

2. schwere Panzerspäh Zug

Panzerjäger Abteilung

In spite of its ever-growing importance, the anti-tank unit was to suffer the most from the reorganizations in 1943–44. In November 1943 it was still organized as earlier in the same year, with three self-propelled Panzerjäger Kompanien equipped with a total of 45 Marder II or III anti-tank SPs supported by three self-propelled 20mm anti-aircraft guns in the leichte Fla Zug, attached to the Stabskompanie. Following the introduction of the 1944 Panzer Division organization, the Panzerjäger Abteilung (other than adding the customary Versorgungs Kompanie) was left with only two self-propelled Panzerjäger Kompanien while the third one reverted to the old motorisiert Zugkraftwagen (motor towed) organization, leaving it with 31 self-propelled Panzerjäger (in theory the new Panzerjäger IV, though one company was often equipped with the Sturmgeschütz) plus 12 towed 75mm PAK guns. In the meantime all the PAK had been withdrawn from every other divisional unit, which produced an imbalance of a dozen anti-tank guns within the division with the total shrinking from 24 to 12, the latter all in the Panzerjäger Abteilung. Since the new KStN did not list the availability of Panzerschreck (they were back with those from 1 November 1944, bringing the total from 174 in November 1943 to the actual figure of 93), apparently the Panzer Division lost a good deal of its anti-tank capability, which could only be partly made good by the

A 150mm schwere Panzerhaubitze SdKfz 165 'Hummel' on the move, apparently towing another vehicle. The sign to the right reads: 'Drive slowly. He who was in a hurry on earth, may find his peace in heaven.' The small symbol at the bottom of the sign is that of a Pionier Brücken Bataillon (bridging battalion).

Panzerjäger Abteilung, 1943–44

1 November 1943

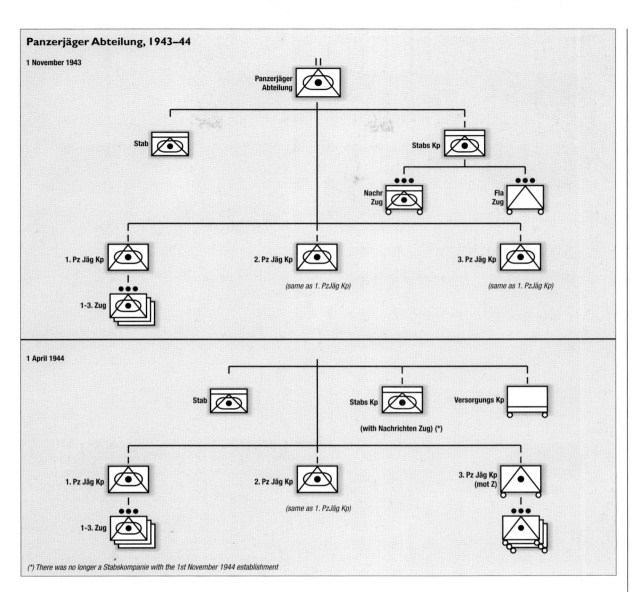

Panzerjäger Abteilung

Stab

Stabs Kp

Nachr Zug

Fla Zug

1. Pz Jäg Kp

2. Pz Jäg Kp *(same as 1. PzJäg Kp)*

3. Pz Jäg Kp *(same as 1. PzJäg Kp)*

1–3. Zug

1 April 1944

Stab

Stabs Kp *(with Nachrichten Zug) (*)*

Versorgungs Kp

1. Pz Jäg Kp

2. Pz Jäg Kp *(same as 1. PzJäg Kp)*

3. Pz Jäg Kp (mot Z)

1–3. Zug

(*) There was no longer a Stabskompanie with the 1st November 1944 establishment

AFVs in a Panzerjäger Abteilung, 1 November 1943

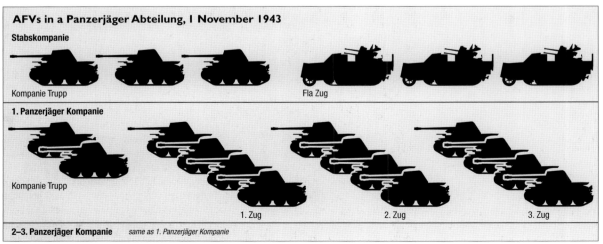

Stabskompanie

Kompanie Trupp

Fla Zug

1. Panzerjäger Kompanie

Kompanie Trupp

1. Zug

2. Zug

3. Zug

2–3. Panzerjäger Kompanie   *same as 1. Panzerjäger Kompanie*

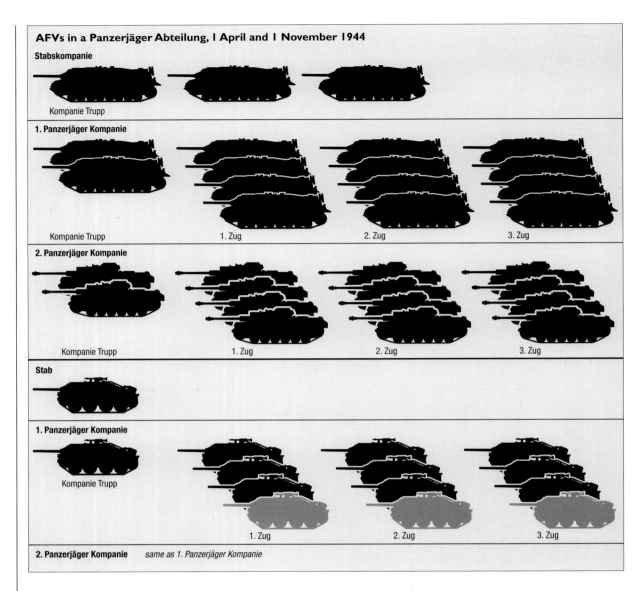

AFVs in a Panzerjäger Abteilung, I April and I November 1944

Stabskompanie

Kompanie Trupp

1. Panzerjäger Kompanie

Kompanie Trupp   1. Zug   2. Zug   3. Zug

2. Panzerjäger Kompanie

Kompanie Trupp   1. Zug   2. Zug   3. Zug

Stab

1. Panzerjäger Kompanie

Kompanie Trupp   1. Zug   2. Zug   3. Zug

2. Panzerjäger Kompanie   *same as 1. Panzerjäger Kompanie*

widespread diffusion of the portable Panzerfaust. The situation worsened in November 1944 since not only was one Panzerjäger dropped from every Zug (the Kompanie Trupp was down to one) but also the Stab, no longer with a Stabskompanie, was reduced down to a single one, thus bringing the grand total to 21 SP guns.

Artillery

The 1943 Panzer Artillerie Regiment granted the Panzer Divisions a greater allowance of firepower than when its I. Abteilung was reorganized as a self-propelled, mixed light and heavy howitzer unit. The Regimental Stabs Batterie included, other than a Nachrichten Zug, a weapons maintenance and a medical section while the Stabs Batterie of every single Abteilung included a Nachrichten Zug, a leichte Fla Trupp with three towed 20mm Flak 38 guns plus an artillery calibration detachment (Artillerie Vermessungs Trupp), supply and trains. Each Abteilung was made up of three Batterien each having either six (in the self-propelled units) or four guns in two Geschütz Staffel; the second Abteilung was equipped entirely with the 105mm leichte Feldhaubitze 18, while the third one

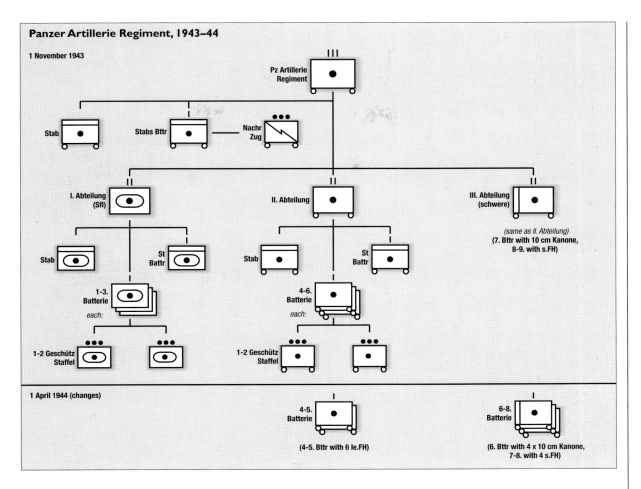

Panzer Artillerie Regiment, 1943–44

1 November 1943

Pz Artillerie Regiment — III

Stab · Stabs Bttr · Nachr Zug

I. Abteilung (Sfl) · II. Abteilung · III. Abteilung (schwere)

(same as II. Abteilung)
(7. Bttr with 10 cm Kanone, 8-9. with s.FH)

Stab · St Battr

1-3. Batterie
each:

1-2 Geschütz Staffel

Stab · St Battr

4-6. Batterie
each:

1-2 Geschütz Staffel

1 April 1944 (changes)

4-5. Batterie

(4-5. Bttr with 6 le.FH)

6-8. Batterie

(6. Bttr with 4 x 10 cm Kanone, 7-8. with 4 s.FH)

was equipped with four 105mm Kanone 18 in the first battery plus eight 150mm schwere Feldhaubitze 18 in the second and third. The first, self-propelled field howitzer (selbstfahrlafette Feldhaubitze) Abteilung provided fully mobile, heavy firepower thanks to its twelve 105mm armed Wespe (wasp) and its six 150mm Hummel (bumble bee) guns mounted either on PzKpfw II or IV chassis which, along with the accompanying Befehl and Panzer Beobachtung (command and armoured observation) tanks and AFVs, was perfectly capable not only of keeping up with all the armoured units of the division, but also of providing closer and more accurate fire support. The reorganization that followed the introduction of the 1944 Panzer Division organization brought some strengths reduction and a few changes; I. Artillerie Abteilung, which maintained its 17 officers and three Beamten, shrank from 135 to 129 NCOs and from 413 to 365 ORs, of which 32 or 16 could be Hiwi. The II. Abteilung, though maintaining its 12 leichte Feldhaubitze 18, was reorganized into two, six-gun batteries thus resulting in an even greater reduction of personnel; its 17 officers shrank to 15 (three Beamten were retained), its 107 NCOs to 89 and its 361 ORs to 267 (with either 20 or 19 Hiwi). The III. Abteilung, on the other hand, only saw a reduction to its other ranks, for it had, in 1943 and 1944, 17 officers, three Beamten, 107 and 109 NCOs and 402 ORs, which shrank to 344 in 1944. All in all, the Panzer Artillerie Regiment was one of the few units to suffer less from the reorganization as it is shown by its vehicle allowance which mainly saw a reduction in the number of lorries from 227 to 167, while half-tracked, non-combat vehicles reduced from 31 to 28. There was no further reorganization in November 1944.

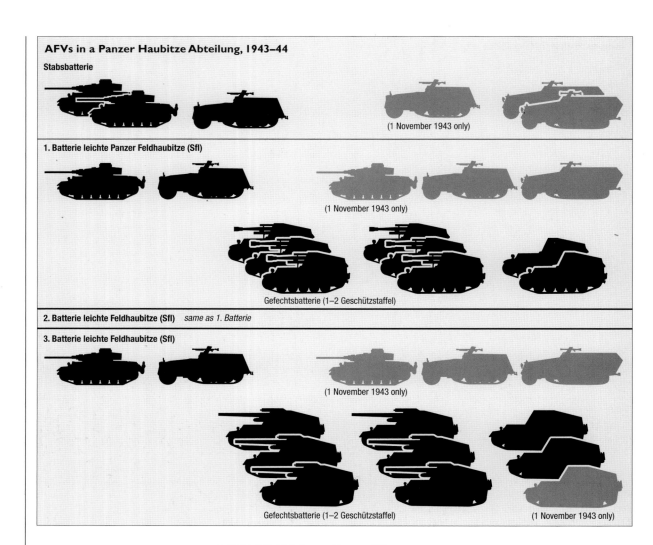

AFVs in a Panzer Haubitze Abteilung, 1943–44

Stabsbatterie

(1 November 1943 only)

1. Batterie leichte Panzer Feldhaubitze (Sfl)

(1 November 1943 only)

Gefechtsbatterie (1–2 Geschützstaffel)

2. Batterie leichte Feldhaubitze (Sfl)   *same as 1. Batterie*

3. Batterie leichte Feldhaubitze (Sfl)

(1 November 1943 only)

Gefechtsbatterie (1–2 Geschützstaffel)   (1 November 1943 only)

Lorries were still badly needed in the last stages of the war, above all for carrying supplies. Their shortage eventually turned into a major shortcoming leading to the pressing into service of all the available types. Early in 1944 Panzer Lehr Division had, for example, 96 different lorry types, 58 per cent of which were produced abroad.

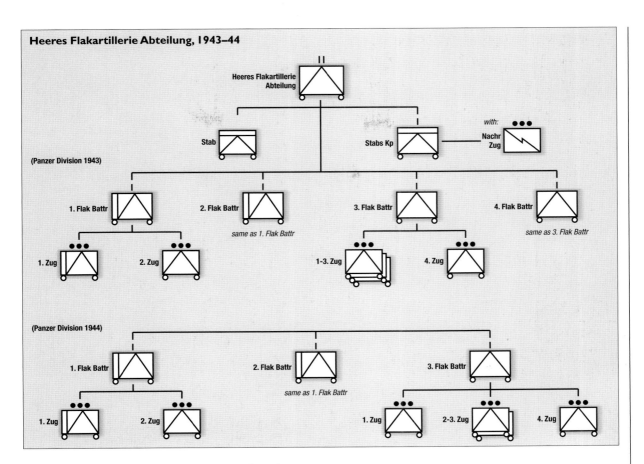

Heeres Flakartillerie Abteilung, 1943–44

In 1943 the Heeres Flak Artillerie Abteilung absorbed the Fla Kompanie formerly attached to the Panzerjäger Abteilung and began to reorganize, a process completed early in 1944; by then its structure included the Stab and Stabs Kompanie, with the Nachrichten Zug plus a supply column (the former leichte Kolonne), and spotting and maintenance units. There were also two heavy Flak Batterien, each with one heavy (four 88mm Flak 36/37 guns) and one light (three 20mm Flak 38) Zug, and two new mixed Flak Batterien 20mm each with three towed (each one with three 20mm Flak 38 guns) and one with a self-propelled (with two four-barrelled 20mm Flakvierling 38/1 on SdKfz 7/1) Zug. Reorganization in 1944 reduced to three the number of the Flak Batterien, the first two still equipped as before and the third one, thanks to the delivery of new equipment, now restructured on a first self-propelled Zug with three 37mm Flak 43/1 mounted on SdKfz 7/2, two towed Züge each one with three towed 37mm Flak 43/1 and a fourth, self-propelled Zug with three 20mm Flakvierling armed SdKfz 7/1.

Panzer Pionier Bataillon

The overall organization of the divisional engineers battalion saw no major changes, though some refinements were still needed. In 1943 it included a Stab and Stabskompanie with an Erkunder and a Nachrichten Zug plus maintenance platoons for vehicles, combat and sappers equipment. The first two Pionier Kompanien, both motorized, had the same organization with their three Pionier Züge plus the MG and Granatenwerfer Gruppe; each one had three officers, 27 NCOs, 180 ORs (four of which could be replaced by Hiwi) and was armed with 152 rifles, 21 MPs, 18 light and two heavy MGs, three Panzerschreck and two 81mm mortars. It had seven cars, 21 lorries, three half-

Panzer Pionier Bataillon, 1943–44

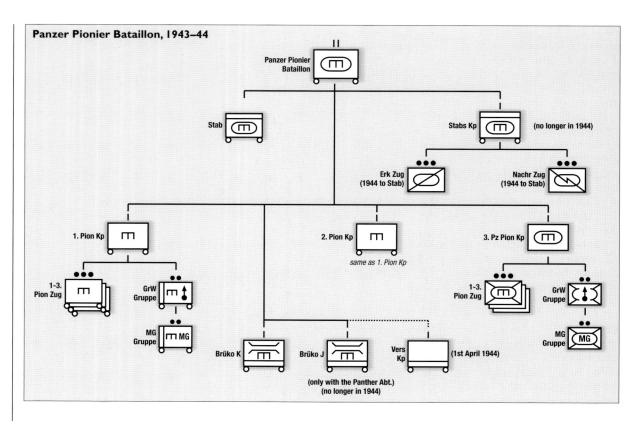

AFVs in a Panzer Pionier Bataillon, 1943–44

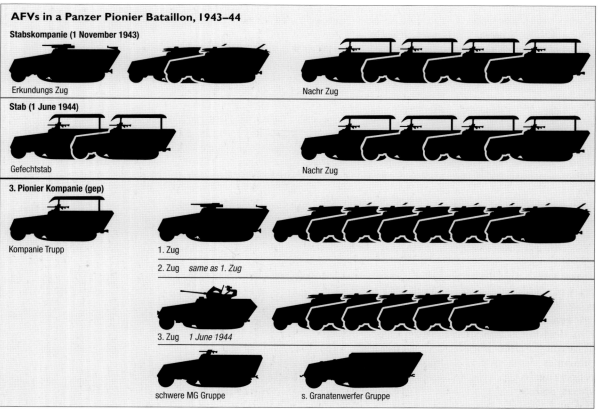

tracks and 11 motorcycles. The third, armoured Pionier Kompanie had the same organization, though it was fully mounted on SdKfz 251 APCs (it had 28 of them, 21 of which were the SdKfz 251/7 engineer version) and had greater strength and firepower with its four officers, 27 NCOs and 199 ORs (seven Hiwi), armed with 88 rifles, 46 MPs, 18 light and two heavy MGs (non-armoured vehicles included one car and 14 lorries).

Even in 1943 the overall organization of the battalion was still quite provisional; other than the customary leichte Panzer Brückenkolonne K (light pontoon column K for tanks), it also included a Brückenkolonne J though only if the division had the Panther-equipped Panzer Abteilung at its disposal. This one was a heavier tank pontoon column with two pontoon and two carrier platoons, plus one light and one support platoon; its total strength was three officers, 31 NCOs, 211 ORs (36 Hiwi) and armament included 218 rifles, two MPs, and five light MGs. It had six cars, 86 lorries, eight half-tracks and 13 motorcycles. As a general rule, it was also escorted by its own Begleitkommando, which had one officer, eight NCOs and 60 ORs, armed with 65 rifles and one MP, though vehicles were only one car and one motorcycle. In 1944 reorganization mainly affected the introduction of the Versorgungs Kompanie and arrangement of the Brückenkolonne K, the only one left, which saw practically no changes to its strength (it had two officers and 14 NCOs in 1943 and 1944, while its 83 ORs shrank to 79 like the Hiwi, from 15 to 12; weapons were either 92 and 81 rifles, while the three MPs and three light MGs of 1943 were retained like the single car, lorries shrank from 37 to 36 and motorcycles from ten to nine). In theory it was to have its own Pionier Zug with one officer, six NCOs, 59 ORs with 62 rifles, one MP, one car and one motorcycle.

Those to suffer most in terms of reorganization were both types of Pionier Kompanie; the motorized ones now had three officers, 26 NCOs and 166 ORs (four Hiwi), with 149 rifles, 21 MPs, 18 light and two heavy MGs, two 81mm mortars, three Panzerschreck, six cars, 14 lorries, five half-tracks and seven motorcycles. The armoured one now had four officers, 29 NCOs, 184 ORs (four Hiwi), 77 rifles, 44 MPs, 18 light and two heavy MGs, two cars, four lorries, six non-combat half-tracks and six motorcycles, while it lost one SdKfz 251/7 from each Zug and replaced the SdKfz 251/10 with the new 20mm gun-armed SdKfz 251/17. Also, the battalion lost its Stabskompanie with the Erkundungs Zug, which was replaced by a Gefechtsstab (combat HQ) put, like the Nachrichten Zug, at direct disposal of the Stab.

Communications and replacements

The 1943 Panzer Division organization of the Nachrichten Abteilung (communications detachment) matched that of earlier the same year, though in this case both the Fernsprech (telephone) and the Funk (radio) Kompanie were partly armoured. The telephone company was in fact made up of four Züge, the first two being equipped with six communication SdKfz 251 (two SdKfz 251/19 for telephone operations in the first Zug, six SdKfz 251/11 for cable laying in the second), and its strength was of four officers, 39 NCOs, 150 ORs (six of which were Hiwi) armed with 175 rifles, 21 MPs and six light MGs and with 15 cars, 20 lorries, one half-track and six motorcycles. The radio company had three SdKfz 251/3 plus two command PzKpfw III in its first Zug and seven SdKfz 251/3 in its second, with a total strength of four officers, 50 NCOs, 200 ORs (four Hiwi) armed with 200 rifles, 25 MPs, six light MGs and with seven cars, 30 lorries, one half-track and six motorcycles.

In 1944 the Nachrichten Kolonne (supply column) was transformed into a Versorgungs Staffel (supply detachment) and both the telephone and radio companies were reorganized. The first one now had only two SdKfz 251/19 in its first Zug and four SdKfz 251/11 in its second, with a total strength of four officers, 35 NCOs, 119 ORs (four Hiwi) armed with 130 rifles, 19 MPs, five light MGs and with 17 cars, 15 lorries, one half-track and six motorcycles. The

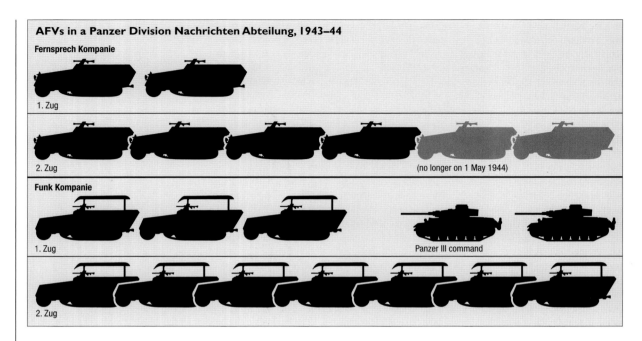

AFVs in a Panzer Division Nachrichten Abteilung, 1943–44

Fernsprech Kompanie

1. Zug

2. Zug

(no longer on 1 May 1944)

Funk Kompanie

1. Zug

Panzer III command

2. Zug

allowance of SdKfz 251 for the Funk Kompanie remained unchanged but its strength did not, falling to four officers, 48 NCOs, 178 ORs (four Hiwi) armed with 184 rifles, 25 MPs, five light MGs and with nine cars, 24 lorries, one half-track and six motorcycles.

The divisional Feldersatz Bataillon (field replacement battalion) was a mere empty shell though heavily equipped with weapons; it served to train replacements which arrived in groups of 200 men for every Marschgruppe (march group) – up to 800 per division at a time. Since these men would only be armed with personal weapons, the battalion had at its disposal not only a good deal of heavy weapons used to train personnel (including one field howitzer, two flamethrowers, one 20mm Flak 38, one 75mm PAK plus one 120mm mortar and one light 75mm Infanterie Geschütz), but it also possessed more automatic weapons than needed (86 MPs, 50 light and 12 heavy MGs), which were used not only for training but also to equip the Marschgruppe. However, such an availability of weapons led several commanders to use the Feldersatz Bataillon as a combat unit in times of need, which would often led to its destruction on the field because of the lack of training and unit cohesion.

Divisional supply and services

Supply for the Panzer Divisions was provided by the Nachschub Truppen (supply troops) under command of the Stab Divisions Nachschub Führer. It had at its direct disposal up to six Kraftfahr Kompanien (motor transport companies) each with a 120-ton capacity, and a Nachschub Kompanie. The actual number and carrying load of the Kraftfahr Kompanie varied according to the availability of motor transport, though the established strength of the 1943 Panzer Division Nachschub Truppen was meant to be 24 officers, three Beamten, 153 NCOs, 819 ORs (161 of which could be replaced by Hiwi) armed with 906 rifles and 52 light MGs and with 45 cars, 340 lorries and 71 motorcycles. With the 1944 Panzer Division the number of Kraftfahr Kompanien fell to five (at times only with a 60-ton load, depending on the availability of lorries) and the Nachschub Kompanie was replaced by a Waffen Instandsetzungs Kompanie (weapons repair company). Total strength was now 21 officers, two Beamten, 119 NCOs and 640 ORs (125 Hiwi), with 707 rifles, five MPs and 40 light MGs and 41 cars, 274 lorries, two half-tracks and 51 motorcycles.

The Kraftfahr Park Truppen (vehicle park troops) provided maintenance to the divisional vehicles; they included two Werkstatt (workshop), one schwere Kraftfahrzeug Instandsetzungs (heavy vehicles repair) Kompanien plus a Nachschub Staffel für Ersatzteile (supply column for spare parts). The total strength in 1943 was seven officers, nine Beamten, 66 NCOs, 357 ORs (81 Hiwi) armed with 365 rifles and 12 light MGs and with ten cars, 63 lorries, seven half-tracks and six motorcycles. In 1944 the strength dropped to 62 NCOs and 338 ORs (75 Hiwi), though the number of rifles eventually rose to 376 (likewise, there were now seven motorcycles), while the number of lorries dropped to 60.

Administrative services were provided by the Divisions Verwaltungs (administration) Kompanie, the Schlachterei (butcher) Kompanie and the Bäckerei (baker) Kompanie which together had a strength of three officers, nine Beamten, 39 NCOs and 200 ORs (26 Hiwi) armed with 230 rifles and equipped with five cars, 34 lorries, one half-track and seven motorcycles. In 1944 these were gathered together in a Verwaltungs Truppen Abteilung and a Stab was added, though overall strength was now reduced to one officer, seven Beamten, 33 NCOs and 192 ORs (26 Hiwi) armed with 216 rifles, three MPs and eight light MGs (a clear sign that now everybody might be called to the front), with five cars, 32 lorries and three motorcycles.

Divisional medical services were provided by two Sanitäts Kompanien (medical companies) and three Krankenkraftwagen Züge (ambulance platoons), with a total strength of 19 officers (physicians and surgeons included), four Beamten, 65 NCOs and 383 ORs (34 Hiwi) armed, in spite of their status, with 396 rifles, nine MPs and seven light MGs and with 15 cars, 93 lorries and 15

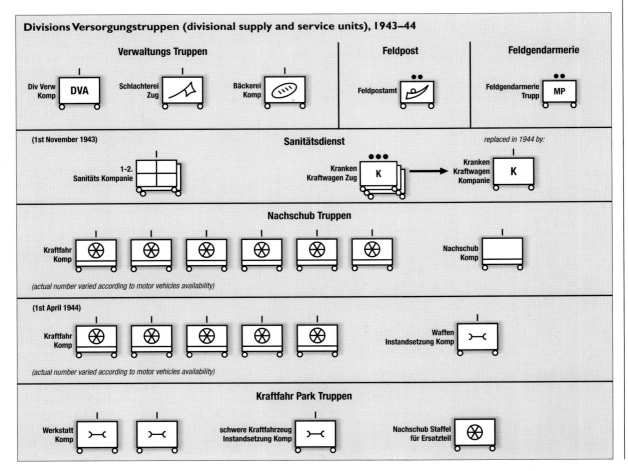

motorcycles. In 1944 a Krankenkraftwagen Kompanie replaced the three Züge; its strength was 17 officers, four Beamten, 86 NCOs and 426 ORs (42 Hiwi) with 460 rifles, 12 MPs and 12 light MGs, plus 16 cars, 85 lorries, 17 half-tracks and eight motorcycles. Both the Feldgendarmerie Trupp (military police unit) and the Feldpostamt (field post office) maintained the same strength in 1943 and 1944; the first had three officers, 41 NCOs and 20 ORs armed with 45 rifles, nine MPs and five light MGs (vehicles included 17 cars, four lorries and six motorcycles), while the second had three Beamten, seven NCOs and eight ORs with 15 rifles, one car and three lorries.

The 1945 Panzer Division

The worsening situation did not prevent the revision and updating of the organization of the Panzer Divisions, though often that simply meant further reductions in strength, weapons, vehicles and equipment. On 22 January 1945 the divisional lorry allowance fell to about 1,200 vehicles, with the divisional supply and services units now down to only 279 lorries. Furthermore, on 25 March 1945 an order was issued to reorganize all the Panzer and Panzergrenadier Divisions (minus the 232. Panzer Division) according to the new 1945 establishment which, in its general outline, included (other than the Begleits Kompanie) a Panzer Regiment now made up of a single Panzer Abteilung and with the second Abteilung replaced by the armoured Panzergrenadier Bataillon, plus two motorized (on paper, since only heavy units were intended to have motor

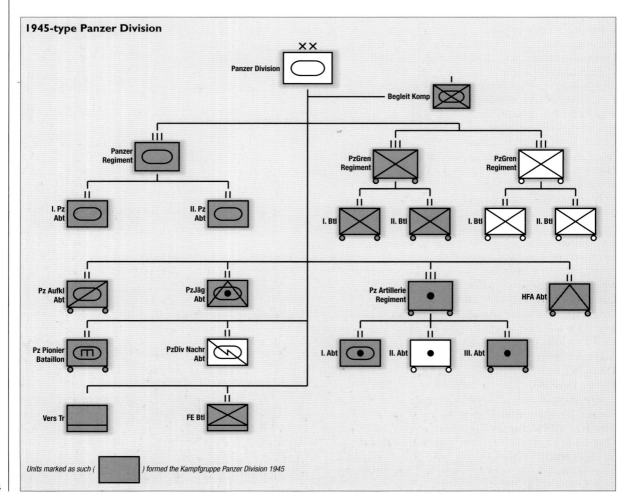

Divisional Kraftfahrpark Truppen (vehicle park troops) provided an essential service to all units by recovering and restoring operational vehicles. In this image a damaged Hummel 150mm self-propelled gun is towed by a Famo F2 SdKfz 9 heavy tractor to the divisional Werkstatt (repair shop), Budapest 1945.

transport) Panzergrenadier Regiments, the Panzer Aufklärungs and Panzerjäger Abteilung, the Panzer Artillerie Regiment, the Heeres Flak Artillerie Abteilung and the Pionier Bataillon, the Nachrichten Abteilung and the Feld Ersatz Bataillon. Overall strength was set at 11,422 all ranks and the division was to have 54 Panzers (Fla and Bergepanzer included – the actual number of combat tanks was 20 Panther and 20 PzKpfw IV), 90 APCs, 16 armoured cars, 22 Panzerjäger, the same allowance of artillery guns and 2,171 vehicles (of which 1,080 were lorries). Those units which, because of their current status, could not be reorganized following these outlines had to reorganize instead according to the '1945 Kampfgruppe Panzer Division' tables of organization, which saw a Panzer Division's combat group being made up of the Begleit Kompanie, the mixed Panzer Regiment, one single motorized Panzergrenadier Regiment, a Panzer Aufklärungs Abteilung down to two companies, the Panzerjäger Abteilung, the Panzer Artillerie Regiment only with its first and third Abteilung, the Heeres Flak Abteilung, the Panzer Pionier Bataillon and one single Nachrichten Kompanie plus the Feldersatz Bataillon and supply and services units.

The total strength of the Kampfgruppe was set at 8,602, though vehicle (including combat vehicle) allowance was the same as for the 1945 Panzer Division. In theory, all commands had to report about the status of their subordinate units by 1 May, though presumably none ever did. It appears that only some divisional units could actually be reorganized according to the new establishment, and only the following divisions are known to have done so – on paper, at least – according to either the 1945 Panzer Division or the 1945 Kampfgruppe Panzer Division organization: 2. Panzer Division (1 April 1945 as Kampfgruppe, after absorbing Panzer Division Thüringen, a training formation), 7. Panzer Division (ordered to reorganize as Panzer Division 1945 on 15 April, to be completed by 1 May), 13. Panzer Division (rebuilt on 31 March 1945 as a 1945 Panzer Division), 16. Panzer Division (ordered on 18 April to rebuild as a 1945 Panzer Division absorbing the Panzer Division Jüteborg), 17. Panzer Division (an 18 April order to reorganize as a Kampfgruppe), 25. Panzer Division (ordered on 25 March to reorganize as a 1945 Panzer Division), 116. Panzer Division (20 April 1945 partly reorganized as a 1945 Panzer Division), and Panzer Division Feld Herrn Halle (to be rebuilt in March as a 1945 Panzer Division). Also, it would seem that 233. Panzer Division (formed on 21 February 1945), Panzer Division Clausewitz (formed 4 April) and Münchenberg (formed 5 March 1945) were organized as 1945 Panzer Divisions.

Divisional medical services played a key role, both during the battle and when at rest. A group of medics poses for a photo in northern Italy in summer 1944; as the symbol on the car's mudguard reveals, they belong to one of 26. Panzer Division's Krankenkraftwagen Züge (ambulance platoons).

Tactics

Salerno, 13–14 September 1943 (16. Panzer Division)

Four days after the Allied landing on the Italian mainland, Hitler ordered Kesselring (C-in-C in southern Italy) to counterattack the enemy bridgehead at Salerno. This was done using both the 16. Panzer and the 29. Panzergrenadier Divisions which, on 13 September, had been facing the US 36th Infantry Division's attack at Altavilla. This was halted and the two battalions of Kampfgruppe Ulich (Panzergrenadier Regiment 15) managed to counterattack, eventually reaching the outskirts of the town. At 4.00 p.m. the same day, on the two sides of the Sele River, elements of both divisions launched the main counterattack taking advantage of a gap in the American defensive line. East of the river the leading elements of Kampfgruppe Krüger (PzGrenRgt 71 and reconnaissance elements of 29. PzGrenDiv) attacked, in cooperation with 16. Panzer Division's Kampfgruppe Kleine-Limberg (Panzer Pionier Bataillon 16 plus elements from Panzer Aufklärungs Abteilung 16), the positions held by US II/157th Regiment and broke through toward the village of Persano, surrounding in the process the I/143rd Regiment and taking some 500 prisoners during the day. At the same time, 16. Panzer Division's Kampfgruppe Döring (Panzergrenadier Regiment 79 supported by 8. Panzer Kompanie with 14 PzKpfw IV and elements from KG Kleine-Limberg) was relieved in its positions south of Battipaglia by Kampfgruppe Stempel (Panzergrenadier Regiment 64) and attacked to the south against the US III/157th Regiment; though achieving a breakthrough, its advance was soon halted in front of the tobacco factory. Other elements did follow along the advance route of KGr Kleine-Limberg, and at 6.00 p.m. LXXVI. Panzer Korps' HQ decided to launch a major attack the following morning with the aim of breaching the American line and driving on to Paestum, in an effort to surround all the enemy forces east of it.

In fact, the German attack took the US VI Corps by surprise and spread panic amongst the defending forces. Not only did the attack at Altavilla end in failure and at a very high cost (I/142nd Regiment was left with about 140 men), but the German breakthrough at Persano and the tobacco factory brought the destruction of II/143rd Regiment, from which only some 300 men returned, and threatened the entire front line. Only heavy artillery fire (some 4,000 rounds that day) managed to prevent any further exploitation. At 7.30 p.m. US 5th Army commander General Clark and the VI Corps commander General Dawley realized they faced a crisis and even considered re-embarking and redeploying the two divisions in the British X Corps area. Nonetheless, both generals decided to hold the line and to withdraw behind La Cosa creek while bringing in more reinforcements, including engineer battalions and the 504th Parachute Regiment, which was airdropped in the Paestum area at night. At 8.00 a.m. on the 14th the German attack was renewed, with the II./PzGrenRgt 79 driving south of the factory to reach the railway line while, to the east of the Sele, other units that were part of KGr Döring, along with most of KGr Kleine-Limberg and elements from the KGr Krüger, drove south trying to get across the Calore River just to the west of Mount San Chirico. Some infantry units actually succeeded in getting across the river supported by 8. Kompanie's PzKpfw IV, but an American counterattack led by the Sherman tanks of A Company, 751st Tank Battalion (withdrawn from Altavilla) prevented a breakthrough and restored the situation. At dusk, the German commanders admitted their infantry were too worn out to

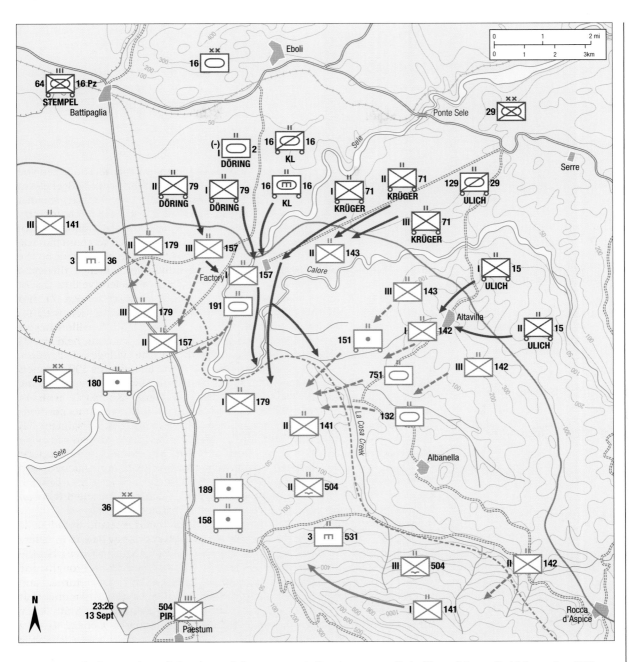

Salerno, 13–14 September 1943

continue with the attack, and the planned thrust towards Paestum was called off. On 15 September Kesselring planned a last counterattack against the bridgehead, which was started the following day, but on the 17th he eventually decided to call every attack off and to start planning a withdrawal north.

Gorodok, 21–27 November 1943 (20. Panzer Division)

Though not much is known about the battles fought on the Eastern Front in the autumn and winter of 1943/44 north of Kursk, these provide a very good example of how the German Army, despite fighting with understrength Panzer Divisions thrown piecemeal into battle, was still capable of dealing

The Germans eventually borrowed from the Red Army the practice of carrying infantry on tanks, thus making up for the lack of vehicles, and keeping them close at hand. This image shows a PzKpfw IV Ausf G of the 3. Panzer Division sporting the insignia (yellow sign on black shield) of Panzer Regiment 6, on the Eastern Front in 1944.

with overwhelming enemy forces (in this case led by incompetent commanders). The offensive on the Kalinin Front started on 6 October with a two-pronged attack against the German defences at Nevel led by the Soviet 3rd and 4th Shock Armies which, after the initial breakthrough, drove respectively to the north and the south, threatening to encircle several units of German 16. Armee and 3. Panzer Armee. In the first week of November the 4th Shock Army crossed the Obol River and began to advance south toward Gorodok and Vitebsk, the latter also under attack from the east on both sides of the Dvina River. The first German reaction was to try to halt the breakthrough at Nevel and, early in November, 20. Panzer Division was sent to counterattack north from Lobok. However, following the Soviet advance and the threat to the rear positions of the German line, the attack (which failed to make any real progress) was called off and 20. Panzer Division was sent south, to Gorodok, once more to deal with a Soviet breakthrough.

20. Panzer Division's task was to hold Gorodok and to keep open a vital line of communication, the north–south road leading to Vitebsk. Moving in a snowstorm and reinforced only by elements of the 113. Infanterie Division (made up of some construction battalions and defence units, though with one Flak and one Sturmgeschütz Abteilung), the leading elements of the division reached Gorodok on the 20th and prepared to counterattack. The city was already defended by elements of the 252. Infanterie Division, though the 4th Shock Army's leading elements had closed in and now stood about 1.5km away, having just captured the woods to the east where a German ammunition depot lay. Lacking armour (the division was only left with the Panzer Abteilung 21 which on 1 November had 20 PzKpfw III and IV), the attack was exclusively led by infantry units; on 21 November Panzer Pionier Bataillon 92 attacked toward the 'Munitionswald' followed on its right shoulder by 112. Panzergrenadier Regiment and on its left by 59. PzGrenRgt. On the first day the Germans managed to seize the 'Munitionswald' and the village of Ssyrownja, though PzGrenRgt 59's drive to Mal. Koscho was pushed back by a Soviet counterattack. A new threat materialized the following day when Soviet infantry supported by some 20 T-34 tanks crossed the lake east of Losswida and closed in on the Vitebsk road; Feldersatz Bataillon 92, which included a Panzer Kompanie (comprising new crews still under training), was the only available force and was sent to deal with it. This was a successful move, since the Soviet drive was pushed back, thanks also to Sturmgeschütz support; the line was restored and the road kept open. Slowly, the German counterattack began to gain momentum; on 23 November III./Infanterie Regiment 7 of 252. Division, with the support of a Panzer Kompanie from Panzer Abteilung 21, attacked toward Schtscherbaki, which was seized three days later. In the meantime, PzGrenRgt 112 attacked toward Ssmoljaki and, along with Panzer Pionier Bataillon 92, to the east toward Lugowzowo, while to the north PzGrenRgt 59 continued its attack toward Mal. Koscho. In poor weather, lacking supplies (the Panzers were eventually forced to fire HE rounds against Soviet tanks since they no longer had any AP rounds) the Germans made slow but steady progress and, by 27 November, a new defensive line was restored along the Lugowzowo–Ssmoljaki–Schtscherbaki area, though south of the Ussyssa River a new Soviet threat materialized in the Lake Beloje area, soon halted by elements of 252. Infanterie Division with Sturmgeschütz support. The Soviet offensive came to a halt and Vitebsk was only seized in June 1944; between 6 October and 31 December 1943 the Kalinin (or First Baltic) Front saw the deaths or disappearance of some 43,500 soldiers, together with 125,000 wounded, out of a strength of 198,000.

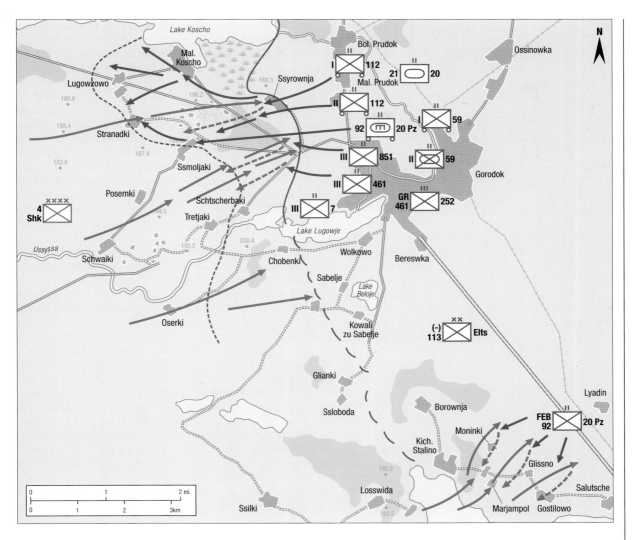

Cherkassy, 16–17 February 1944
(1. Panzer Division)

Gorodok, 21–27 November 1943

Both Salerno and Godorok offer good examples of the classic Panzer Division counterattack, in the first case trying to wipe out an enemy beachhead with a breakthrough followed by an envelopment manoeuvre, in the second case by restoring a defence line taking some key positions from the enemy. Cherkassy provides quite a different example, since in this case the counterattack was only aimed at one single purpose: to relieve encircled German forces. The Soviet offensive in the southern part of the Eastern Front, which started between late September and mid-October 1943, by late December had created a large German bulge on the southern Dniepr bend between Zitomir and Zaporoze. The new offensive, which began on 23 December 1943 east of Kiev and in the Kirovograd area, saw portions of both German 1. Panzer and 8. Armee in a bulge still protruding north, with its front running along the Dniepr; with a swift attack, in four days the Soviet 1st and 2nd Ukrainian Fronts (with some 336,000 men, 524 tanks and SP guns, 5,300 artillery pieces and heavy mortars) encircled the remnants of six understrength German divisions, only one of which, the 5. SS-Panzer Division 'Wiking' (with the attached Sturmbrigade 'Wallonie') did not exclusively consist of infantry. All in all, some 54,000 German soldiers were trapped. Following Hitler's orders, Von Manstein decided to launch a counterattack with the aim of relieving the forces in the pocket and restoring the situation, at least as far as possible, though of the nine Panzer Divisions initially envisaged for the operation only four (3, 11, 13 and 14. Panzer Divisions) were able to attack on 1 February 1944, though with a total strength of only 58 Panzer and Sturmgeschütze and a total infantry strength of 3,795. Only with the arrival of the III. Panzer Korps did the real attack start, on 4 February; temperatures rose causing the snow to melt, leading to the beginning of the 'muddy season'. Other than four divisions (16, 17 and 1. Panzer Divisions plus the 1. SS-Panzer Division 'Leibstandarte'), the corps' trump card lay in the schwere Panzer Regiment Bäke. Formed in January and made up of the schwere Panzer Abteilung 503 and the II./Panzer Regiment 23 (their strength was then 34 Tiger and 46 Panther tanks), the brilliantly led unit had already proved itself during the relief of the Uman pocket, when in the space of a week it destroyed some 268 enemy tanks for the loss of four of its own. However, the effects of the muddy season heavily influenced its capabilities – moving in the mud forced a Panther to consume its entire fuel tank (730 litres) to cover just 3.5–4km. Mud slowed down the advance and only on 8 February did the 16. Panzer Division establish a bridgehead on the Gniloj Tikic River, from where the second phase of the attack was started again on the 11th, now with a total tank strength of only 149 Panzers and Sturmgeschütze.

The 30-odd kilometres between the bridgehead and the pocket soon turned into hell not only because of the mud, which also added problems with supplies (on 13 February some 61 cubic metres of fuel and 34 tons of ammunition were airdropped to solve the problem), but also because of the Soviet defences. To face German counterattacks, often with an armoured spearhead, the Soviets had in fact developed 'anti-tank gun front' tactics, which saw the employment of anti-tank and artillery guns dug in along the most favourable areas to halt the German advance, thus enabling Soviet tanks to counterattack. Losses were therefore heavy on both sides; while on 13 February alone the Germans destroyed some 100 Soviet tanks and SP guns, on the 15th the 1. SS-Panzer Division was left with only three Panzers and one operational Sturmgeschütz. On 15 February, a last order was issued to both the 1. Panzer Division, whose Kampfgruppe Frank (Panzer Regiment 1 with armoured elements from II./PzGrenRgt 1 and II./113 plus Panzer Pionier Bataillon 37 and II./Artillerie Regiment 73) was now III. Panzer Korps' spearhead, and to the encircled forces clearly stating that the pocket was to be evacuated starting on the night of 16/17 February, following the advance to point 239 – which was to be the meeting point. On the very same day I./Panzer Regiment 1 and II./PzGrenRgt 113 entered Lisjanka in spite of a solid Soviet defence; Panzer Regiment Bäke could not cross the river with its Tiger tanks, but was nonetheless able to support the attack of II./PzGrenRgt 113 (actually consisting of 50–60 men) and of the four Panthers of 1. Kompanie Panzer Regiment 1 against Oktjabr, which was only taken in the afternoon of the 16th. German units were so understrength (II./PzGrenRgt 113 was left with 10–12 men per company, I./Panzer Regiment 1 only had 12 Panthers) that even the small Kampfgruppe Heimann (with fewer than 100 men) from 1. SS-Panzer Division was needed to support KGr Frank's attacks on Hill 239. Yet, in spite of repeated attacks, it was still in enemy hands when the encircled German units began to move out of the pocket heading west at 11.00 p.m. on the 16th. It was thanks to Bäke and his Panzer Regiment that the hill was finally taken; after a delivery of fresh supplies, with skilled and bold leadership the regiment (with eight Tiger and six Panther tanks operational), supported by Panzer Aufklärungs Abteilung 16, attacked Chizincy and turned south towards Hill 239, which was taken in the morning of 17 February without problems. Eventually, more than 36,000 men succeeded in escaping the trap, though III. Panzer Korps paid the price with 559 dead, 347 MIA and 2,252 wounded plus the loss of 156 Panzers and Sturmgeschütze. The Soviets in turn lost 80,000 men and 606 tanks.

Targul–Frumos, 2 May 1944
(24. Panzer Division)

After Kursk the Germans not only lost the strategic initiative, but at the tactical level they mainly reacted to enemy actions, often with poor results. Counterattacks led by the Panzer Divisions lacked now all the elements that had characterized the early years of German armoured warfare: the concentration of forces, manoeuvre, speed and flexibility. At best, they could achieve no more than temporary gains, like restoring the line or allowing encircled forces to escape a trap and, as at Salerno, they seemed no longer capable of driving deep into enemy-held territory. Therefore, in spite of the fact that both Soviet and Allied forces still operated according to schematic patterns, the Germans could still countermanoeuvre with inferior forces thanks to their superiority in command, control and communications. Based on the Kampfgruppe concept, the main shortcoming in this system was the lack of vehicles (especially AFVs) and equipment, which led to the creation of armoured/motorized Kampfgruppen, often lacking the necessary strength to do anything more than face, albeit effectively, enemy attacks. In May 1944 LVII. Panzer Korps defended a sector of the front in Moldavia in the Targul–Frumos area, relying mainly on the Panzergrenadier Division 'Grossdeutschland' (on the front line) and, in reserve, the depleted 24. Panzer Division. Its two Kampfgruppen, one made up of the armoured elements (Von Waldenburg with III./Panzer Regiment 24, I./PzGrenRgt 26, PzAA 24 acting as a light Panzergrenadier battalion and I./Artillerie Regiment 89) and the other one (Von Einem with II./PzGrenRgt 21 and II./PzGrenRgt 26) had only 25 per cent of their vehicles and 60 per cent of their infantry combat strength left, plus only 24 serviceable PzKpfw III and IV. Nonetheless, when on 2 May the Soviet 24th Tank Corps started its attack in the Ulmii–Liteni area, which soon led to a breakthrough in the defence line of Füsilier Regiment 'GD' and to an armoured drive toward Facauti and Targul–Frumos, 24. Panzer Division was promptly called to counterattack and restore the defence line.

Given the terrain, a decision had to be made whether to counterattack either north or south of the Fadarjesal depression; in the latter case, it would have been hard to regain the lost ground while, in the former one, the counterattack might have faced the Soviet defensive anti-tank gun front on the Belcesti ridge. The forces were therefore split, with KGr von Waldenburg attacking north of the river and KGr von Einem moving to the south, were it was to prevent a major Soviet breakthrough toward Targul–Frumos. At about 11.00 a.m. KGr

A Panther commander is shown talking to the crew of an SdKfz 251 Ausf D, in the summer of 1944. Panzer crews used the cumbersome earphones, plus the throat mike, shown in this photo, until September 1944, when the new set called 'Funkhaube A' (which could be used when wearing a steel helmet) was introduced.

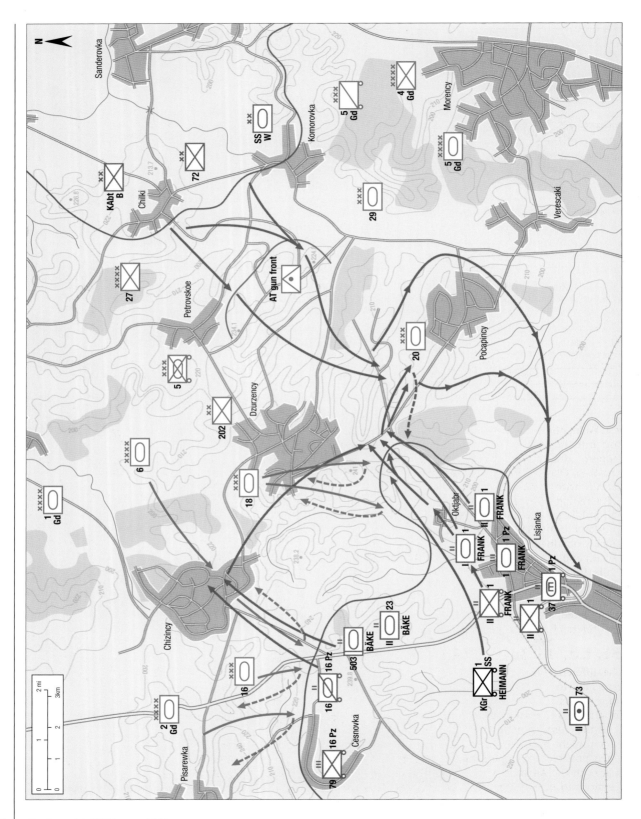

N

Sanderovka

Morency

Komorovka

Verescaki

Pocapincy

Okljabr

Lisjanka

Chilki

KAbt
B

72

SS
W

4
Gd

5
Gd

5
Gd

29

27

AT gun front

Petrovskoe

20

5

Dzurzency

202

6

18

1
Gd

FRANK
1

FRANK
1

FRANK
1

FRANK
1

1 Pz

1 Pz

37

Chizincy

BÄKE

BÄKE
23

503
16 Pz

16

16

16

16 Pz

79

Cesnovka

KGr
1
SS
HEIMANN

73

2
Gd

Pisarewka

2 mi

3km

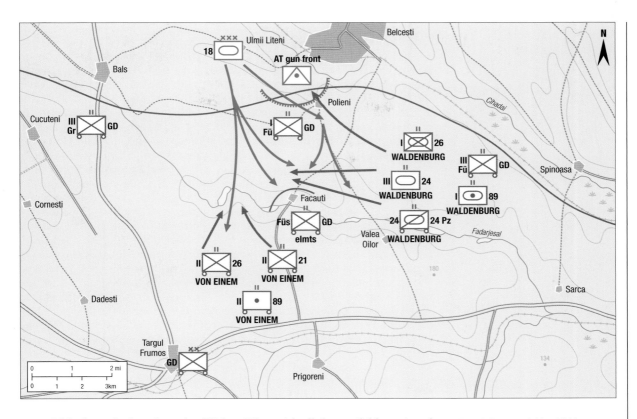

von Waldenburg deployed north of Valea–Oilor, with all the available anti-tank and anti-aircraft guns ready to defend the area and the artillery set to fire on request; after a brief reconnaissance and a personal appreciation of the situation, Oberst von Waldenburg decided to counterattack the Soviet drive at Facauti with the Panzer and the Panzer Aufklärungs Abteilung while the I./PzGrenRgt 26 was to drive north to make contact with the German forces still holding the line in the Polieni area and, above all, to deal with the Soviet anti-tank front. The attack started early in the afternoon and success was quickly obtained; in half an hour a dozen or so Soviet tanks were destroyed in Facauti and PzAA 24 was able to drive the enemy infantry away from the town, while I./PzGrenRgt 26 reached Polieni and opened fire on the ridge, thus effectively preventing enemy AT and artillery from firing at German tanks and vehicles moving south. At the end of the day the enemy breakthrough had been halted, and the whole of 24. Panzer Division prepared to launch a major counterattack, which eventually restored the front line.

St. Lo, 11 July 1944 (Panzer Lehr Division)

The differences between the Eastern and the Western fronts soon became clear, especially to the men of the Panzer Divisions; in the East, in spite of their improved skills and capabilities, Soviet forces were still unable to react promptly to German counterattacks because of the rigidity of their command structure. Also, in early 1944 the Soviets did not have similar air superiority, which might have prevented the Germans from redeploying their forces and, when possible, regrouping them in strength. On the West, it was soon clear that both the Americans and the British forces were perfectly capable of swift reactions to meet any threat and, above all, that they had full air superiority. As a consequence, the type of counterattacks that might have been successful against the Red Army rarely achieved anything against the Allies. More than a month after the Allied landings in Normandy no major counterattack had been launched by the Panzer Divisions, which now faced strong pressure from the Americans against their positions in front of St. Lo.

The Panzer Lehr Division ('Lehr' were demonstration units used to experiment with new tactics and weapons) was at times the best division of the German Army; with a total strength of 14,700 it was fully mechanized with all the four Panzergrenadier and the Panzer Pionier Bataillone mounted on SPW (the division had 658 of them plus 35 in short-term repair), plus a full complement of 99 PzKpfw IV, 89 Panther (from I./PzRgt 6), 31 Jagdpanzer IV and 10 Sturmgeschütz III, plus 10 Tigers from the attached Panzer Kompanie 316 (a unit equipped with remote-control destruction vehicles). Not all units were sent to Normandy, notably Panzer Kompanie 316, but fighting against the British forces in June cost the division severe losses: 490 killed, 1,809 wounded and 673 missing in action. On 1 July it had only 36 PzKpfw IV ready for action plus another 29 in short-term repair, 32 and 26 Panthers and 28 and 9 Jagdpanzer and Sturmgeschütze. Even before redeployment in the St. Lo area, the division was ordered to attack the positions held by 9th and 30th US Infantry Divisions, supported by the 3rd Armored Division, with the aim of seizing the bridge on the Vire–Taute canal north of St. Jean de Daye. The intention of General von Choltitz, commander of LXXXIV. Armee Korps, was for this to be a swift action in two stages – first breaking through the enemy lines then, with all the Panzergrenadiere and Pioniere aboard their vehicles, a dash to the river before the enemy could react. Reality soon intervened; the attack, scheduled for 9 July, had to be delayed because the Panzer Lehr was unable to promptly redeploy due to the poor conditions of the roads, which were badly bomb damaged and under heavy air attack (movement took mainly place at night). Also, the lack of aerial reconnaissance did not permit the German commanders to realize the Americans had reinforced their lines and were ready to face any threat. As a result, the four Panzergrenadier and two Panzer battalions of the Panzer Lehr had to face 21 American infantry and nine tank and tank-destroyer battalions.

The doomed attack was not uneventful; moving early in the morning from Point Hebert, Bataillon Kuhnow attacked supported by 8./PzRgt Lehr, breaking

A Kampfgruppe of Panzer Lehr Division is ready to move to the front in Normandy, June 1944. In the foreground is an early Panther Ausf D, while in the background a late-production model, and behind it a heavily camouflaged SdKfz 251, can be seen. On the right, some Panzergrenadiers and a tank crew are discussing the situation.

through the positions of the 119th Infantry Regiment, though its reserves and the 823rd Tank Destroyer Battalion eventually managed to halt the German drive before Bahois, well short of the objective of Cavigny. To the left, Hauptmann Böhm's II./PzGrenRgt 902 and 7./PzRgt Lehr soon had to abandon their attack against Le Rocher, which was heavily defended by III/120th Infantry Battalion with the support of the CCB of the 3rd Armored Division. In the beginning, the situation was better on the other side; Bataillon Philipps (I./901) easily broke through the III/39th Infantry Regiment positions at Le Desert and about 9.30 a.m. reported it had taken many prisoners and was moving forward. However, 1./PzRgt 6's leading Panthers were destroyed and blocked the road; when the last one was destroyed as well all the others were lost. II./PzGrenRgt 901 had better luck with its drive to La Charlemenerie, where American infantry and tank destroyers soon halted its march. At 11.00 a.m. the American counterattack began and Panzer Lehr's attack was called off. It had cost 700 men, 10 Panther and eight PzKpfw IV tanks.

Caen, 18 July 1944 (21. Panzer Division)

By 11 July 21. Panzer Division had lost 3,411 men out of the 16,297 it had on 1 June and, on 17 July, it had 50 PzKpfw IV left. Deployed south-east of Caen, the division was ready to face a new British attack, though no one could foresee the hell that the start of Operation 'Goodwood' would unleash on 18 July. The attack plan was simple in its conception; their path opened by air bombardment, three armoured divisions were to advance east of Caen then switch west to surround the city and gain access to the plains beyond. Starting at 5.30 a.m., 4,500 bombers in three waves bombed pre-selected areas, a move immediately followed by a massive artillery and naval bombardment. In spite of narrow roads, congested by some 750 tanks and 8,000 vehicles funnelling their way across their own and the enemy's minefields, at 7.30 a.m. precisely the 11th Armoured Division's 29th Armoured Brigade took the lead and started to advance with the 3rd RTR, 23rd Hussars and 2nd Fife and Forfar Yeomanry, crossing the German defence line and meeting no opposition from the stunned men of 16. Luftwaffe Feld Division. A quarter of an hour later, 159th Infantry Brigade, supported by the tanks of the 2nd Northamptonshire Yeomanry, began to advance toward Cuverville and Demouville. Both the 29th and 159th Brigades made good progress, slowed occasionally by craters and roads that existed no longer; at about 9.00 a.m. the 3rd RTR crossed the railway between Demouville and Banneville, heading to Frementel. Yet, in spite of their losses, four batteries of Sturmgeschütz Abteilung 200 (deployed at Giberville, Le Mesnil, Le Prieure and Grentheville) managed to have some operational vehicles partly deployed in support of I./PzGrenRgt 125, which established a defence line at the crossroads north of Le Mesnil, and partly in support of the II./PzGrenRgt 125, which created its own defence line at Emieville. All were part of Kampfgruppe von Luck, formed around Panzergrenadier Regiment 125.

Panzergrenadiers and Sturmgeschütz tanks took position at Le Mesnil at about 10.00 a.m., just before the Shermans of the 3rd RTR approached the village – at which point everything started to go wrong for the attacking force. At Cagny, untouched by the air bombardment, were four 88mm Flak guns, which opened fire against the advancing Shermans of the 3rd RTR and 2nd Fife and Forfar, who were masking the town rather than trying to seize it, quickly destroying 16 of them. When the 29th Brigade approached Le Mesnil the German defenders fiercely opposed its repeated assaults and it took an hour, until 11.00 a.m., for the village to be taken. Also, the 159th Brigade, which at 10.15 a.m. had easily seized Cuverville, got stuck while attacking Demouville; the latter was eventually seized only at 2.30 p.m. Thus, in spite of the fact that now the 5th Guards Brigade, followed by the 32nd Guards Brigade (both delayed by traffic jams), was advancing along the path of the 29th Brigade, the

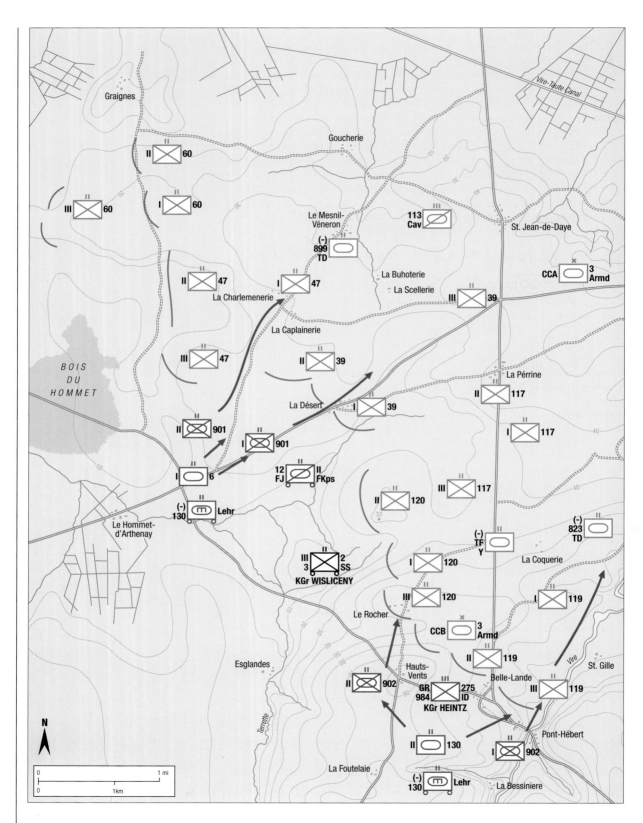

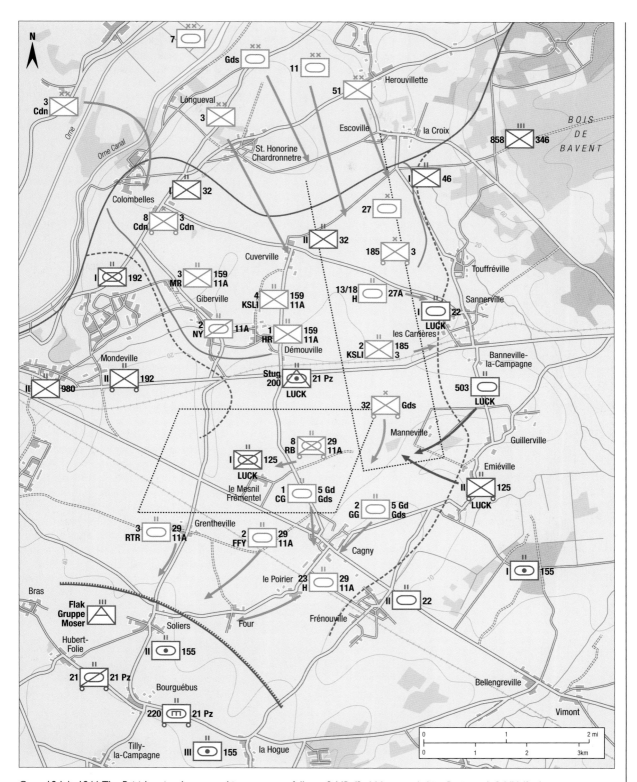

Caen, 18 July 1944. The British units shown on this map are as follows: 3 MR (3rd Monmouthshire Regiment), 2 NY (2nd Northamptonshire Yeomanry), 4 KSLI (4th King's Shropshire Light Infantry), 1 HR (1st Herefordshire Regiment), 13/18 H (13/18th Hussars), 2 KSLI (2nd King's Shropshire Light Infantry), 8 RB (8th Motor Battalion, the Rifle Brigade), 1 CG (1st Coldstream Guards), 2 GG (2nd Grenadier Guards), 3 RTR (3rd Royal Tank Regiment), 2 FFY (2nd Fife and Forfar Yeomanry), and 23 H (23rd Hussars).

latter was left without infantry support and was unable to clear the German-held positions. Precious time was lost, and the Germans were able to recover and prepare their defences. At about noon remnants of schwere Panzer Abteilung 503 (badly shaken by the bombardment) attacked from Emieville, along with II./PzGrenRgt 125; the leading elements of the Guards Armoured Division were quite careful in approaching Cagny. In the meantime the 29th Brigade probed south across the railway toward the Bourguebus ridge, only to find it was heavily defended by units of 21. Panzer Division untouched by the bombardment and by the Flak guns. The advance stalled, and in early afternoon nearby units from 1. SS and 12. SS-Panzer Divisions begun to arrive in the area, further consolidating the German defences. Although 'Goodwood' did not come to an end until 22 July, by which point most of the ground south of Caen had been captured, it all but ended on its very first day when the advance of the 11th and Guards Armoured Divisions was stalled by the tenacious German defenders, who, on 18 July alone, destroyed 126 and 60 tanks respectively of each unit.

Arracourt, 25–29 September 1944 (11. Panzer Division)

The situation was slightly better for the Panzer Divisions when they faced Allied forces after their breakout from Normandy; the latter's problems with supply and fatigue, and difficulties with air support in wooded areas, helped to tip the balance once more in favour of the Germans, in spite of the heavy losses suffered. In late September 1944 the 11. Panzer Division (deployed in southern France to face the Allied landings of 15 August, and then subsequently withdrawn north) was not only short of its established strength, but was also only left with some 50 tanks until 24 September, when it absorbed the remnants of Panzer Brigades 111 and 113. The following day, the division started its attack against the US 4th Armored Division's salient at Arracourt, one of Patton's 3rd Army's wedges into the German defensive lines in Lorraine. An initial German drive on Moyenvic on the 24th soon revealed the town was not occupied, so II./PzGrenRgt 110 continued to advance and the following day all other units started to attack American-held positions, until the CCA of the 4th Armored was ordered to withdraw from the Juvelize salient to create a shorter, easier to defend line. The withdrawal was completed by 26 September; the 4th Division was now mainly holding the line with infantry units, against which 11. Panzer Division's attacks continued all through the 27th, when a new major offensive was started against the southern shoulder of the salient. A diversionary attack was launched by II./PzGrenRgt 111 and I./PzRgt 15 (which

The SdKfz 162 Jagdpanzer IV was the first to be produced of the new generation of 'tank hunters'. Armed with a 75mm L/70 gun, it was at first intended for use by Panzerjäger Abteilung, though, from November 1944, it could also be used to replace the PzKpfw IVs in the newly formed mixed Panzer Abteilung.

A typical PzKpfw IV in 1944, with its three-colour camouflage, armour skirts and Zimmerit paste. By this date it was rarely seen on the Eastern Front following the appearance of the Soviet T 34/85 and Josef Stalin tanks, but it was still a match for the American Sherman and the British Cromwell tanks on the Western Front.

had about 20 tanks left) at Bezange la Petite, which they seized; however, they proved unable to advance any further because of the fierce opposition from the 10th Infantry Battalion and elements from the 702nd Tank Destroyer Battalion. Likewise, II./110 and I./PzGrenRgt 111's drive to Xanrey was halted by American fire and a quick counterattack by the 53rd Infantry and 35th Armored Battalions. To the south, the main attack led by I./PzGrenRgt 110 and PzAA 11, supported by some 25 tanks previously from Panzer Brigade 113, drove through American-held lines, but was soon halted in front of Hill 318, where the fighting continued over the following days. Although limited support was given to the German attackers by II./PzGrenRgt 110, moved to the south, the artillery (which was repositioned) failed to show and the reappearance of the American fighter-bombers – which on the 28 performed 107 sorties – eventually compelled 11. Panzer Division's units to seek rest. A last, desperate attack on the 29th was met with low-flying P-47 fighters and it was called off when the German units began to panic. Energetic measures were needed to restore the situation yet, in spite of the fact that the attack ended with failure, in that sector Patton's 3rd Army advance had been halted.

A rear view of a PzKpfw V Panther Ausf D/A on a sunken road typical of the Normandy battlefield, June–July 1944. The bocage terrain in Normandy, with its trees and hedge-lined roads and fields, was well suited to infantry defence. However, it denied the German AT guns the advantages of long-range use and greater accuracy.

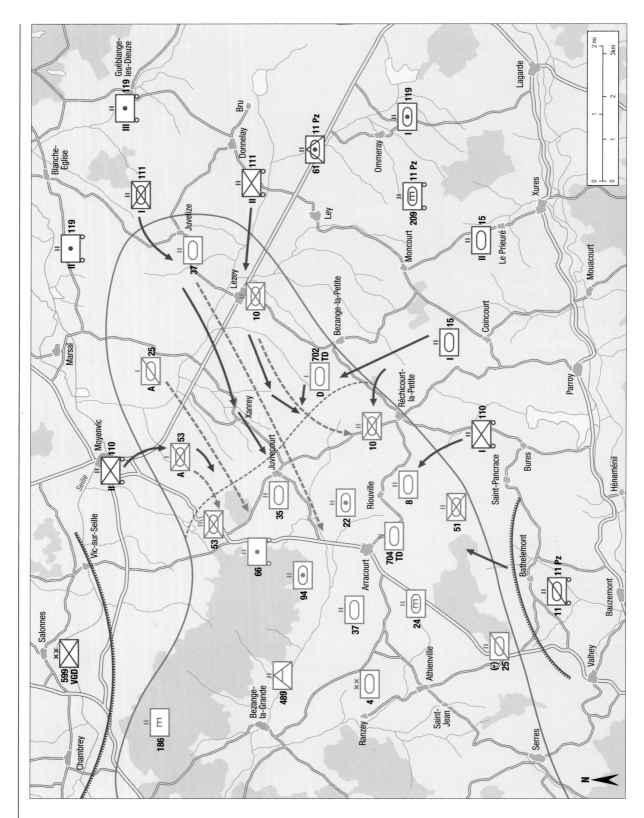

Nyiregyhaza, 26 October 1944 (1 and 23. Panzer Divisions)

Following Romania's defection to the Allies in August 1944, the few German forces that escaped annihilation were trapped in a large bulge protruding south into the Transylvanian Alps. A slow withdrawal began, while Soviet forces attacked to the west towards Belgrade and to the north towards Debrecen. In late October the last German forces were leaving the bulge, their escape route closed at times by the Soviets. On 26 October the Soviet 7th Mechanized Corps managed to drive through the German lines and seize the vital crossroad of Nyiregyhaza, while the 6th Guards Cavalry Corps attacked the German forces from the south. 23. Panzer Division was ordered to rescue them, regaining Nyiregyhaza and establishing a link with the withdrawing 3. Gebirgs Division. An armoured Kampfgruppe was organized with Panzer Regiment 23 (with three Panther, four Sturmgeschütz and one PzKpfw IV tanks) and Panzer Aufklärungs Abteilung 23, the only SPW-mounted unit, supported by the self-propelled guns of I./Panzer Artillerie Regiment 128, while PzGrenRgt 126 was to follow and PzGrenRgt 128 was to secure the southern shoulder at Hajdu-Dorog. Attack started at 9.00 a.m. and within a couple of hours the river west of Nyiregyhaza had been crossed; rather than waiting for PzGrenRgt 126 to arrive, the Kampfgruppe continued its march and by noon one company from PzAA 23 supported by two Sturmgeschütze was in the town, having taken the enemy forces completely by surprise. In the meantime Panzer Aufklärungs Abteilung 1 had attacked from the south, where 1. Panzer Division's Panzergrenadier

Nyiregyhaza, 26 October 1944

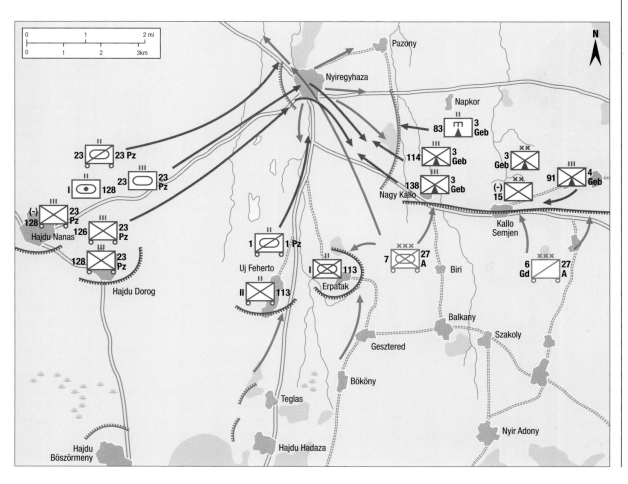

Regiment 113 was holding the villages of Uj. Feherto and Erpatak against the 7th Mechanized Corps' attacks; the apparently demoralized Soviet troops withdrew south leaving the crossroads in German hands. Meanwhile, Gebirgsjäger Regiment 138 and 144, with Gebirgs Pionier Bataillon 83, attacked from the bridgehead at Nagy Kallo and by early afternoon had managed to break through the enemy defence lines; at 4.30 p.m. the leading elements of 23. Panzer Division from the west and 3. Gebirgs Division from the east met up. The escape route was opened up again and at dusk 3. Gebirgs Division took over the defences of Nyiregyhaza from 23. Panzer Division. Five days later the last German forces withdrew from the bulge.

Hürtgen Forest, 2–9 November 1944 (116. Panzer Division)

The American 28th Infantry Division attack towards the Roer River dams started surprisingly well, with II/112nd Infantry easily seizing Vossenack on the very first day (2 November) while III/112nd and I/112nd seized – to everybody's surprise – Schmidt and Kommerscheidt respectively on the 3rd. Actually theirs was an easy task against the remnants of German 275. Infanterie Division defending the area, while the northern and southern shoulders experienced stiff resistance moving against elements of 89. Infanterie Division and the incoming units of 116. Panzer Division. These took up their positions after moving during the night of 3 and 4 November, ready to counterattack 28th Division's breakthroughs in the morning; facing the same problems of bad weather and unsuitable terrain, the two divisions began a fierce struggle. On 4 November Panzergrenadier Regiment 156, supported by elements of Panzer Aufklärungs Abteilung 116, attacked the eastern edge of Vossenack under cover of artillery fire; after nine hours the attack was called off without any result, the Americans still holding their positions. 272. Infantry Division's units had better luck attacking Schmidt from the north-east; I and III./Infanterie Regiment 1055, supported by Sturmgeschütz Brigade 341, attacked at 10.45 a.m. eventually compelling the III/112nd Infantry Regiment to withdraw. In the afternoon of 4 November Regiment 1052 attacked Kommerscheidt along with III/Infanterie Regiment 860 and II./Panzer Regiment 16, the latter with nine PzKpfw IV. Badly prepared and poorly led, the attack ended in failure and five German tanks were lost. The hard fighting continued. On 5 November the 28th Division commander, General Cota, sent Task Force Ripple, including elements of 707th Tank Battalion and III/110th Infantry Battalion, along the Kall River trail to Kommerscheidt to help the defenders of I/112nd. The movement was hindered by Panzer Aufklärungs Abteilung 116, which controlled the ridge to the east of Vossenack and Kommerscheidt; TF Ripple's men got through, but theirs was not an easy task.

A destroyed Flakpanzer IV Wirbelwind. This particular variant of the PzKpfw IV-mounted Flakpanzer was produced using those PzKpfw IV which had returned from the front for major overhauling. Production ceased in November 1944 since the Flakvierling 38/1 was not as effective as the 37 mm Flak 43.

Under German tank and anti-tank fire, by 6 November only six tanks and three tank destroyers were still operational in Kommerscheidt. On the very same day, a crisis arouse in Vossenack; a surprise attack led by Panzergrenadier Regiment 60, with II/PzGrenRgt 156 and other elements from the division, eventually broke through the American defences. Panic spread, and thanks only to the intervention of the 146th Engineers the situation was somehow restored, though half of the town was now in German hands. Again on the 6th, elements of 89. Infanterie Division were used to create a Kampfgruppe led by Panzer Regiment 16's commander (Oberst Bayer), which on the following day led the attack of Infanterie Regiment 1055 supported by the remnants of Panzer Regiment 16 and

Sturmgeschütz Brigade 341, while PzAA 116 secured the area between Vossenack and Kommerscheidt. The crucial day of the battle was 7 November; after a bitter fight, American troops evacuated Kommerscheidt, eventually creating a defence line along the Kall River, while in Vossenack the 146th Engineers counterattacked clearing the eastern tip of the town. The fighting continued on a much smaller scale on 8 and 9 November, when both sides took a badly needed rest, though only a few units of 116. Panzer Division could be withdrawn for refitting (five weeks later the division took part in the Ardennes offensive). The American 112nd Infantry Regiment had lost 2,093 men, about one third of the 6,184 lost by the 28th Division during the battle.

Celles–Rochefort, 23–26 December 1944 (Panzer Lehr, 2. Panzer Division)

Although doomed from its very outset, the Ardennes offensive did at least prove that the Panzer Divisions were still able to perform like they did in the early blitzkrieg years of the war. The only difference was that they were no longer facing the same enemy. Returning to the concepts of manoeuvre, speed and flexibility, on 22 December Kampfgruppe von Böhm (2. Panzer Division's Panzer Aufklärungs Abteilung 2), moved through a breach in the American positions between Marche and Rochefort at Hargimont and, with a daring march, got to Buissonville and Achene, which it reached at nightfall on the 23rd. The last dash took the Kampfgruppe to Foy Notre Dame, from where it pushed forward down to the village of Drehance – less than ten kilometres from the final objective: the Meuse River. A few hours behind KGr von Böhm, a second Kampfgruppe from the 2. Panzer Division, KGr von Cochenhausen (which had changed its commander the day before), followed on the same path; made up of Panzergrenadier Regiment 304 and I/PzRgt 3, plus two artillery battalions with Pionier and Flak units, it reached Hargimont moving then to Humain, Buissonville and directly to Petite Trisogne until reaching Celles. Shortly after nightfall, while KGr von Böhm and Cochenhausen closed on the Meuse, further to the west Panzer Lehr's Kampfgruppe von Poschinger (Panzergrenadier Regiment 902 with two companies from II/PzRgt 130) approached Rochefort, a vital road junction to the west. The place was defended by the 3/335th Infantry Regiment with one anti-tank company plus a tank destroyer and engineer platoon which, lacking strength, were unable to prevent the Germans from sneaking into the town under cover of darkness at 2 a.m. on the 24th. House-to-house fighting ensued in the central area of the town until, at 1.00 p.m., American troops were ordered to withdraw, which they did by 6.00 p.m. With German troops close to the Meuse and a road opened up to their rear, from which both the Panzer Lehr and 2. Panzer Division could start marching to the west, for a moment – and leaving aside problems of supply and enemy air superiority – it was almost like being back in May 1940.

However, in 1944 the enemy was no longer an army with a slow, inadequate command system, but rather a modern army capable of reacting in a timely fashion. On the night of 23 December, as the leading elements of 2. Panzer Division approached the Meuse and those of Panzer Lehr Division approached Rochefort, the American 2nd Armored Division moved south to counter the German advance. On the morning of 24

A Panzergrenadier is shown cleaning his MP 40 submachine gun. In 1944 some Army Panzergrenadier units, particularly in the West, not only had a better allowance of automatic weapons but were also issued camouflaged uniforms in greater quantity like the one worn by this soldier, thus matching their Waffen-SS counterparts.

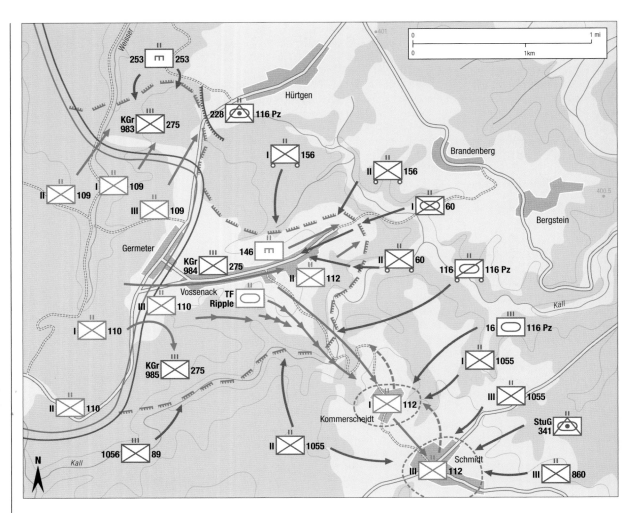

The Hürtgen Forest, 2–9 November 1944

December Combat Command A took up position north-east of KGr von Böhm and Cochenhausen at Leignon, while CCB arrived at Ciney just to the north. Its forces split into two task forces (A and B), CCA then advanced to Buissonville, which was seized in the afternoon, halting the advance of Kampfgruppe von Fallois (Panzer Aufklärungs Abteilung 130 from the Panzer Lehr) and the elements of KGr von Poschinger probing from Rochefort. Meanwhile, the British 29th Armoured Brigade, with the 3rd Royal Tank Regiment in the lead, was deployed to screen the approaches to the Meuse replacing the US 1st Army provisional regiment. All of a sudden, in spite of the fact that three other Panzer Divisions were closing in to join 2. Panzer and Panzer Lehr Division, the weakness of the German positions became clear. On Christmas day, while the 82nd Armored Reconnaissance linked up with the British 29th Brigade, 2nd Armored Division's CCB split into two task forces and moved south against KGr von Cochenhausen and von Böhm. Practically surrounded, lacking supplies (above all fuel), they faced up to the American forces as best they could, hoping for relief. However, 9. Panzer Division's closing in on Hargimont was slowed down by lack of supplies, the Panzer Lehr was facing 2nd Armored CCA at Buissonville (to be joined on the 25/26 by CCR) and the only available force that could be put together was Kampfgruppe Holtmayer, which was 2. Panzer Division's Panzerjäger Abteilung 38 reinforced by the remnants of a Panther company. Before it could start its march, on the 25th KGr von Böhm was destroyed with the loss of 148 men; a few others managed to escape to join KGr Cochenhausen. In the night of 25/26 December

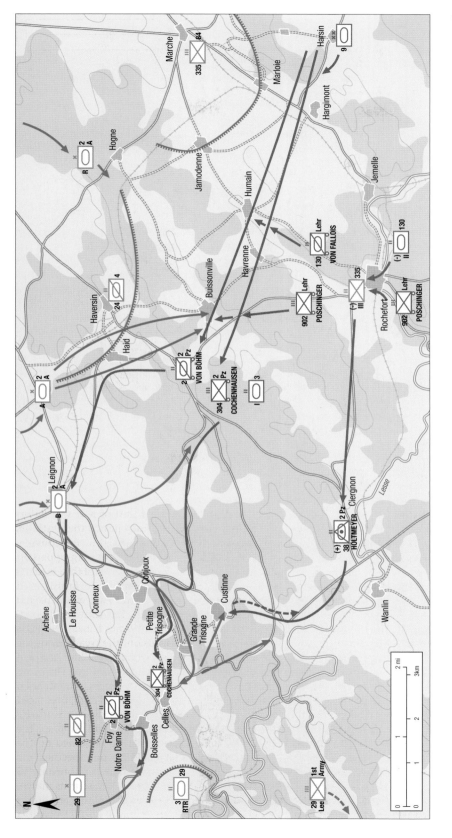

KGr Holtmeyer assembled near Rochefort and moved west to Ciergnon, although its progress was slowed by contact with patrols from 2nd Armored's CCA. In late morning KGr Holtmeyer approached Custinne, only to face I/67th Armored Regiment and a hail of fire from American artillery and air attacks. By early afternoon the Kampfgruppe came as close as 800m to the pocket, though its men were exhausted. Eventually the order to pull back arrived and some 800 men, including KGr commander Major von Cochenhausen, managed to escape from the pocket to join KGr Holtmeyer on its way back. 2. Panzer Division not only failed to reach the Meuse, but lost most of its Panzergrenadier Regiment 304 plus the bulk of its Panzer Aufklärungs Abteilung 2 and most of Panzer Regiment 3 and Panzer Artillerie Regiment 74.

Wissembourg, 8–9 January 1945 (21. Panzer Division)

Operation Northwind, a poor relation of the Ardennes offensive, started on 31 December 1944 against the American positions in Alsace; lacking all the resources of the latter, above all surprise and armoured support, it only achieved limited gains. It was not a true offensive but rather a series of multi-divisional attacks, taking place in the same area of the front; the Americans could only allocate limited resources against this, and they therefore planned to counter the enemy threat with a series of staged withdrawals. One of the most critical moments for the Americans came early in January 1945, when Heeresgruppe G (Army Group G) decided to launch its armoured reserve, made up of 21. Panzer and 25. Panzergrenadier Division, against the Lautebourg salient to break through the American defences and drive to the Hagenau Forest to try to link up with the southern arm of the offensive aimed at Strasbourg. The area was defended by the US 42nd Infantry Division, a green one which had arrived in France only in December, and by Task Force Linden (313rd Infantry Regiment) of the experienced 79th Infantry Division. Actually, 21. Panzer Division (the leading armoured force) was in little better shape since on 1 January its strength was only 14,600, 2,600 short of the established one, mobility was only 40 per cent and it only had nine PzKpfw IV (plus 17 in short-term repair) and 31 Panthers (plus two in short-term repair). Its task was made harder by its lack of preparation; since the American troops had taken up a defensive line running along the fortifications of the Maginot Line, the commanders asked for detailed maps and intelligence reports, both of which were unavailable. The division assembled at Wissembourg on 5 January and the following day started its drive south, facing a determined and fierce resistance from the American 222nd Infantry Regiment. After two days of fighting, the Germans managed to reach a point from which they could start the real offensive, as the higher command had requested. In the bitter cold and falling snow, on 8 January Kampfgruppe von Luck (Panzergrenadier Regiment 125), with its II Bataillon in the lead and supported by Sturmgeschütz Abteilung 200 (with 20 newly arrived Jagdpanzer tanks) and I./Panzer Regiment 22, attacked Task Force Linden's positions west of Stundwiller, on the Maginot Line fortifications. Although the element of surprise was missing, since the men of TF Linden had spotted the German soldiers approaching, the men of KGr von Luck managed to break through the American positions with the help of armoured support, eventually reaching the village of Oberroedern. However, to the north Panzergrenadier Regiment 192 was unable to break through the American defences of 222nd Infantry Regiment south of Ingolsheim. Only early in the morning of the following day, 9 January, did the men of 25. Panzergrenadier Division meet with success; they surprised the green troops of 42nd Division deployed in the fortifications around Hatten, succeeded in breaking through the first line of defence and seized the town. This success eventually enabled KGr von Luck to continue its advance towards Hoffen, though the fact that 25. Panzergrenadier Division's advance was halted at Rittershoffen made the German breakthrough a very limited one. Kampfgruppe von Luck eventually turned to Rittershoffen, where a fierce struggle imposed a delay, which enabled US 14th Armored Division to reach the area. The battle raged for another 10 days, until the Americans eventually withdrew – though the Germans still failed to achieve a breakthrough.

Stuhlweissenburg, 20–21 January 1945 (1. Panzer Division)

The equivalent of the Ardennes offensive on the Eastern Front was Operation Konrad, launched on 1 January 1945 in an attempt to relieve the forces encircled at Budapest and which ended on the 27th some 15km short of its objective. The last offensive (Konrad 3) began on 17 January 1945 to the south of Budapest and, though lacking surprise, a breakthrough was soon achieved. In the night of 18/19 January the leading unit of 1. Panzer Division, II./PzGrenRgt 113, overcame the Soviet defences at Urhida and managed to establish a bridgehead on the Sarviz Canal, though the damaged bridge could not be used for the heavy Panther tanks until the Pioniers repaired it late on the 19th; to the south, I./PzGrenRgt 113 managed to establish another bridgehead at Falubattyan. Patrols reported that enemy forces, part of the Soviet 21st Guard Corps, had withdrawn east of the canal and therefore, in the night of 19/20 January, Kampfgruppe Philipp (Panzer Regiment 1 with its I Abteilung and I./PzRgt 24 supported by I./Artillerie Regiment 73) crossed the canal and moved ahead; the Grenadiers of II./PzGrenRgt 113 were carried on Panther tanks while KGr Weber (SPW mounted I./PzGrenRgt 113) followed. At dawn a Soviet anti-tank gun position running along the Stuhlweissenburg–Falubattyan railroad was quickly overwhelmed and eventually silenced by the men of KGr Weber, which then turned south to establish a defence line on KGr Philipp's right shoulder (the bridges were defended by elements of Panzerjäger Abteilung 37). Taking advantage of the situation, Philipp decided to continue his advance east while II./PzGrenRgt 113 dismounted and attacked Stuhlweissenburg, defended by elements of the Soviet 20th Guards Corps, managing to enter its southern suburbs. At dusk, Philipp's tanks easily broke through another Soviet defence line on the Stuhlweissenburg–Seregelyes road, which therefore became unusable by the Soviets for their own supplies. On the night of 20/21 January 1. Panzer Division's Panzergrenadier Regiment 1 started crossing the canal and moved east toward Stuhlweissenburg, where also elements of 23. Panzer Division and Kampfgruppe Ney (a regimental-sized combat group made up of Hungarian SS soldiers attached to 5. SS-Panzer Division 'Wiking') were approaching from the north-west.

Aware that the rest of the division was following and having realized that Soviet forces were only able to set up small and uncoordinated counterattacks, Philipp decided to take a risk and to continue with a night advance, supported only by a few Grenadiers from II./PzGrenRgt 113 and by I./Artillerie Regiment 73. Under cover of darkness the Kampfgruppe reached Dinnyes, on the south-west corner of Lake Velence. The Soviet positions were stormed by the Panthers of I./PzRgt 24 – only six in total, since all the others had been left behind because of mechanical breakdowns caused by the poor conditions of the terrain. The surprise was such that during the night Soviet supply lorries continued to arrive in the town, only to be 'taken into custody' by the Germans. Taking further advantage of the element of surprise, at dawn on 21 January Philipp took command of the tanks still in working order and dashed along the southern edge of the lake, before being halted by elements of the Soviet 5th Guards Cavalry Corps at the village of Kapolnasnyek, on its south-eastern edge. That same night Stuhlweissenburg was attacked by the other units of 1. Panzer Division and KGr Ney, and was eventually seized on the morning of 22 January.

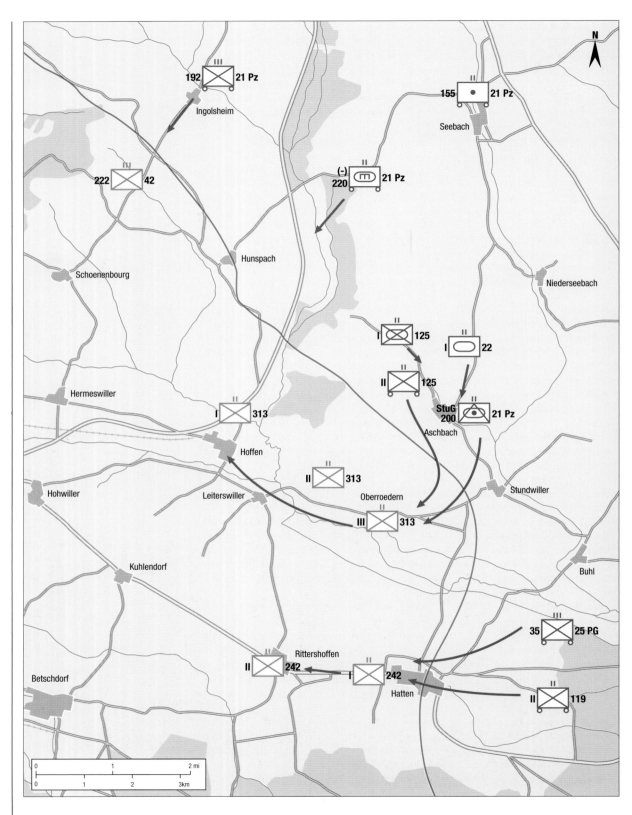

N

192 21 Pz

Ingolsheim

155 21 Pz

Seebach

222 42

(-)
220 21 Pz

Schoenenbourg

Hunspach

Niederseebach

I **125**

I **22**

II **125**

Hermeswiller

I **313**

Hoffen

StuG 200 21 Pz

Aschbach

Stundwiller

Hohwiller

Leiterswiller

II **313**

Oberroedern

III **313**

Buhl

Kuhlendorf

35 25 PG

Betschdorf

II **242**

Rittershoffen

I **242**

Hatten

II **119**

0   1   2 mi

0   1   2   3km

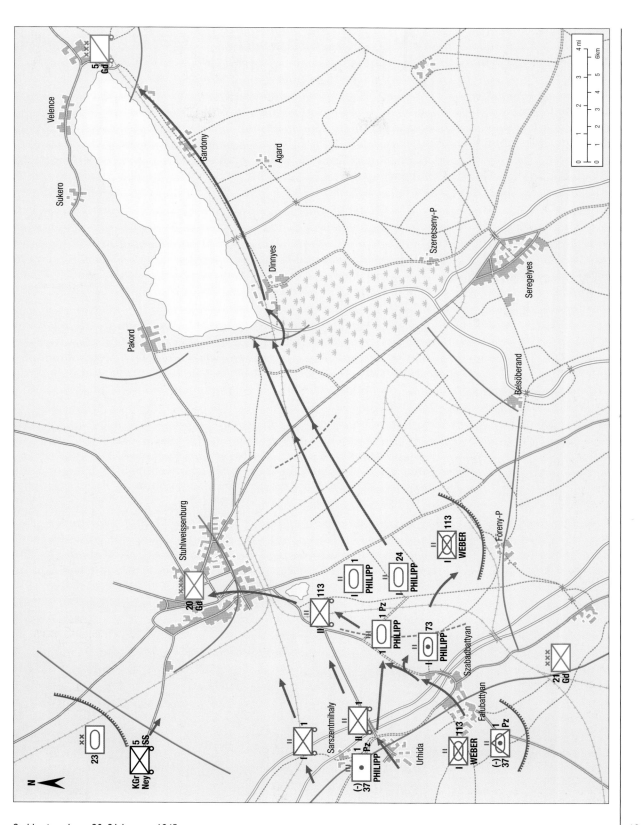

Velence

Sukero

Gardony

Agard

Dinnyes

Pakord

Szerecseny-P

Seregelyes

Belsöberand

Stuhlweissenburg

Förény-P

WEBER
113

PHILIPP
1

PHILIPP
24

20
Gd

113

1 Pz

PHILIPP
1

PHILIPP
73

Szabadbattyan

21
Gd

23

5
SS

KGr
Ney

Sarszentmihaly

1 Pz
PHILIPP

Uhida

WEBER
113

Falubattyan

(-)
37
1 Pz

(-)
37

N

Weapons and equipment

In the final two years of the war, the Panzer Divisions were much stronger than previously, not only because of changes to their establishment, but also thanks to the issue of improved weapons and equipment. The latest versions of the PzKpfw IV tank made it a match for enemy tanks, while the Panther often proved superior to them. New infantry anti-tank weapons like the Panzerschreck and the Panzerfaust helped the Panzergrenadiers deal with enemy armour more effectively, and, thanks to the new array of SdKfz 251 and 250 armoured support vehicles, the infantry now had better mobility and support. New Panzerjäger tanks and the increased availability of self-propelled artillery also provided direct and incisive support to combat units. However, in 1944 the tank was still the master of the battlefield. German statistics dealing with anti-tank warfare on the Eastern Front from January to April 1944 clearly show there was no real alternative to the Panzer as an effective weapon to face enemy armour; in January 38.2 per cent of the 3,670 enemy tanks whose fate had been ascertained (out of a total of 4,727 actually destroyed) were destroyed by Panzers, 28.6 per cent by anti-tank guns, 20.6 per cent by Sturmgeschütze and Panzerjäger, 9.5 per cent by mines and artillery and 3.1 per cent by infantry in close combat. There were some variations in the three months that followed; out of 1,905 tanks recorded as destroyed in February (out of a total of 2,273 actually destroyed) 44.8 per cent had been destroyed by Panzers, 17.9 per cent by PAK, 24.8 per cent by Sturmgeschütze and Panzerjäger, 7.7 per cent by mines and artillery and 4.8 by the infantry. Of the 1,031 tanks destroyed in March (out of 2,663 actually destroyed) 11.8 per cent had been destroyed by Panzers, 31.7 per cent by PAK, 28.8 by Sturmgeschütze and Panzerjäger, 13.8 by mines and artillery and 13.9 by infantry. The trend, apparently shifting in favour of the Sturmgeschütz, the Panzerjäger and the infantry eventually reversed its course in April, when 53.2 per cent of the 1,542 tanks destroyed (out of 2,878) were destroyed by Panzers, 16.3 per cent by PAK, 15.3 per cent by Sturmgeschütze and Panzerjäger, 4.1 per cent by mines and artillery and 11.1 per cent by infantry. Some comparisons are possible with a report dated 29 June 1944 giving tank kills on the Normandy front; in this case 227 (42.3 per cent) out of the 537 reported enemy tanks killed had been destroyed by Panzers, 84 by towed anti-

A PzKpfw V Panther Ausf A of I./Panzer Regiment 4 in Italy in 1944. Starting in early 1943, one of the two Abteilungen of the Panzer Divisions' Panzer Regiment was sent back to Germany to re-equip with Panther tanks, but many of them would never rejoin their parent units and were rather sent where the need was greater.

tank guns (15.6 per cent, plus another 21 by Flak, bringing the total to 19.6 per cent), 61 by Sturmgeschütze and Panzerjäger (11.4 per cent), 36 by artillery (6.7 per cent, probably also including mines) and 108 by infantry in close combat, which is 20 per cent. Although simply indicative these figures heavily imply that Panzer took always the lion's share of tank kills, while anti-tank guns (either towed or self-propelled) added a valuable contribution. Infantry anti-tank capabilities, still quite limited in early 1944, apparently improved during the year though it is hard to say how much this was due to portable anti-tank weapons or more favourable terrain. In any case, the fact remains that in 1944 anti-tank guns, land defences, artillery and the new infantry anti-tank weapons could support the Panzers, but could not replace them.

From July 1943 German tank production grew both in quantity and in quality; in the second semester (excluding light and heavy tanks) the output was 1,746 PzKpfw IV and 1,284 PzKpfw V Panthers – about 37 per cent more PzKpfw IV and about 40 per cent more Panthers than in the first half of the year. The definitive shift in favour of the PzKpfw IV, of which 3,225 samples (plus 36 Bergepanzer IV, 96 Beobachtungs Panzer IV and 97 PzBefh IV) were produced in 1944, is clear if we consider that in the same period Panther production stood at 3,777 samples (plus 227 Bergepanzer V). Worth noting, in 1941 German overall tank production was 3,256, which included five different types of tanks. In the first four months of 1945 some 438 PzKpfw IV (plus three Bergepanzer and 31 Beobachtungs Panzer) and 507 Panthers (plus 38 Bergepanzer) were produced. Panzers recovered by maintenance services should also be added, since these stood at 973 in October 1943, 911 in November, 1,294 in December and 2,190 in January 1944 (plus another 280 recovered in Germany). These figures notwithstanding, German armour production proved unable to bridge the gap with the enemies and consequently the German field tank inventory was never able to cope with the ever-increasing enemy superiority. Indeed, a simple look at the actual field tank strength reveals a dramatic situation; in July 1943 German overall tank strength (taking only into account the types in use with the Panzer Divisions) included 1,423 PzKpfw III, 1,472 PzKpfw IV and 428 Panthers. In August 1943 the figures stood at 1,244 PzKpfw III, 1,374 PzKpfw IV and 524 Panthers. In December 1943 the German Army still had 960 PzKpfw III (920 in January 1944) compared with 1,689 PzKpfw IV (1,668 in January 1944) and 912 Panthers (1,084 in January 1944); in June 1944, a critical month, the Panzer inventory included 839 PzKpfw III, 2,304 PzKpfw IV and 1,898 Panthers. In November 1944 there were still 523 PzKpfw III (none at the front), 1,605 PzKpfw IV (1,630 in December) and 1,729 Panthers (1,966 in December). Only in September did the Panther overtake the PzKpfw IV, with 2,135 compared with 2,110. In February 1945 the inventory included 1,491 PzKpfw IV and 1,964 Panthers.

Since these figures show gross totals, including reserves and training tanks, the actual strength at the front was much lower, while losses were often quite impressive. On 31 July 1943, after the battle of Kursk, the actual Panzer strength on the Eastern Front (excluding Tiger, command and flamethrower tanks) was 1,684. This figure included 728 PzKpfw III, 710 PzKpfw IV and 134 Panthers; on 10 July the actual strength in Sicily was 130, which included 52 PzKpfw III and 78 PzKpfw IV. This makes a grand total of 780 PzKpfw III with field units out of the 1,423 in the inventory, 788 PzKpfw IV out of 1,472 and 134 Panthers out of 428. On 20 August 1943 there were 1,519 Panzers on the Eastern Front including 555 PzKpfw III, 687 PzKpfw IV and 178 Panthers. In Italy there also were 477 Panzers including 67 PzKpfw III, 335 PzKpfw IV and 71 Panthers, for a grand total of 657 PzKpfw III (out of 1,244), 1,022 PzKpfw IV (out of 1,374) and 249 Panthers out of 524. The situation only partially improved on 31 December 1943 with 1,461 Panzers on the Eastern Front, including 196 PzKpfw III, 841 PzKpfw IV and 349 Panthers, 145 PzKpfw III, 316

A stopgap measure to improve air defence for the Panzer Regiment: the Flakpanzer 38 (t). Based on the PzKpfw 38 (t) chassis, it was armed with a single-barrelled 20mm Flak 38 which was not so effective against the enemy air threat. Mostly employed in Normandy, it was replaced by the heavier Flakpanzer IV.

PzKpfw IV and 157 Panthers on the Western Front, and in Italy a total of 263 Panzers (no breakdown is available, though we know the figures do not include the Panther). Even at this stage only 506 Panthers out of the 912 available were either at the front or in threatened areas, at a time when its serviceability rate eventually increased from four to 31 per cent. Also, not only were a relatively low number of Panzers deployed at the front, but the actual availability was further curtailed by heavy losses.

Since production proved unable to cope with the losses suffered, newly produced tanks were mainly used to either rebuild depleted units or to create new ones; replacements for the Panzer Divisions at the front were always scarce. Total losses in the second half of 1943 amounted to 534 PzKpfw III, 1,481 PzKpfw IV (nearly 85 per cent of production) and 525 Panthers, 40.9 per cent of those produced in the same period. Although most of these losses occurred on the Eastern Front (85 to 90 per cent in summer 1943), replacements only amounted to 1,197 Panzers (heavy and command ones included) plus 526 of all types that were part of individual companies and battalions (the figures do not include tanks with the Panzer Divisions transferred to the Eastern Front). Since some 2,500 of the 3,042 Panzers were lost on the Eastern Front (including light, heavy, command and recovery types), clearly 1,723 replacements could neither fill the gap nor help to reduce the growing imbalance with the Red Army. That could only be done thanks to the arrival of fresh Panzer Divisions on the Eastern Front; in October 1, 14 and 24. Panzer Divisions helped the actual tank strength to recover from its all time low, but, in the meantime, attrition took a heavy toll on the Panzer Divisions fighting on the Eastern Front. 7. Panzer Division, which fought in its southern portion until mid-1944, had a total tank strength of 81 tanks on 1 July 1943 (seven PzBefh, seven PzKpfw II, 29 PzKpfw III, 38 PzKpfw IV), which dropped to 35 on 1 October (three PzBefh, three PzKpfw II, nine PzKpfw III, 20 PzKpfw IV) and only rose to 41 on 1 December 1943 (two PzBefh, one PzKpfw II, seven PzKpfw III, 21 PzKpfw IV). On 1 February 1944 its tank strength stood at 32 (one PzBefh, three PzKpfw III, 28 PzKpfw IV) and only on 1 June was there a partial recovery, when 7. Panzer Division had 43 PzKpfw IV. In the central portion of the Eastern Front, 20. Panzer Division was in not much better shape; on 1 July 1943 its tank strength stood at 50 (15 PzKpfw III and 35 PzKpfw IV), dropping to 24 on 1 October (five PzKpfw III and 19 PzKpfw IV); on 1 December it had 31 tanks (two PzKpfw III and 29 PzKpfw IV) rising to 46 on 1 February 1944 (three PzKpfw III and 43 PzKpfw IV) and eventually to 63 on 1 June (seven PzKpfw III and 56 PzKpfw IV). The contrast with 1. Panzer Division, which arrived on the Eastern Front in late October 1943, is striking, since on 1 December its tank strength stood at 115 (74 PzKpfw IV and 41 Panther); on 1 February 1944 the division still had 76 tanks (40 Pzkpfw IV and 36 Panthers), though on 1 June its tank strength dropped to 58 (34 PzKpfw IV and 24 Panthers). Quite clearly in spite of production, which peaked in 1943–44, the Panzer Divisions never fully recovered their strength and instead suffered heavily from attrition.

Germany's strategic situation was another influential factor; from late 1943 the growing concerns about the Allied invasion of North-West Europe brought changes to the overall strategic pattern which had seen depleted units sent there for rest and refitting before being sent back to the Eastern Front. Thus five out of the six Panzer Divisions (including two Waffen-SS) deployed in the West in July 1943 were sent to other fronts in the months that followed and, in June 1944, only one of them (21. Panzer Division) was left, eventually joined by eight other Panzer Divisions (including three Waffen-SS ones) which were either forming (Panzer Lehr since March, 116. Panzer Division since May) or being rebuilt (2. Panzer Division since February, 9. Panzer Division since May, 11. Panzer Division since June; 19. Panzer Division was stationed in the West between June and August 1944, while 25. Panzer Division was in Denmark). One of the consequences of the new strategic pattern was a steady growth in total tank strength on the Western Front since December 1943; the 656 Panzers then available (including 145 PzKpfw III, 316 PzKpfw IV and 157 Panthers) turned into 1,039 (including 99 PzKpfw III, 587 PzKpfw IV, 290 Panthers) in February, while in April tank strength stood at 1,403 (including 114 PzKpfw III, 674 PzKpfw IV and 514 Panthers) eventually reaching the figure of 1,552 on 10 June (of which 39 were PzKpfw III, 748 PzKpfw IV and 663 Panthers; about 1,100 of these Panzers were deployed in France and Belgium). On 31 May 1944 tank strength on the Eastern Front was about 1,200 medium and heavy tanks, including some 680 PzKpfw IV and 313 Panthers. In summer 1944 it mattered little what kind of achievements German tank production obtained, since available resources were already spread over two main fronts as well as the Italian. Losses also grew during these months, when the German army suffered many, serious defeats; in the first half of 1944 overall losses amounted to 2,505 tanks, of which 124 were PzKpfw III, 1,177 PzKpfw IV and 752 were Panthers. From July through to September 1944 another 2,625 tanks were lost, including 1,086 PzKpfw IV and 923 Panthers. This time, with almost every Panzer Division engaged at the fronts, new production was used to make up for losses; in June and July 1944 a grand total of 573 PzKpfw IV out of the 602 produced during these months were sent to the front as replacements to make good the loss of 695 tanks of the same type (266 lost on the Eastern Front, 347 replacements; 274 lost on the Western Front, 152 replacements; 155 lost in Italy, 74 replacements). Also, another 644 Panthers out of the 750 produced in June and July 1944 were used as replacements to make good the loss of another 513 (258 lost on the Eastern Front, 236 replacements; 207 lost on the Western Front, 370 replacements; 48 lost in Italy, 38 replacements). The situation did not change in September, clearly reflecting a change in overall strategy; 315 PzKpfw IV out of the 480 produced in August–September (300 plus 180) were sent as replacements to the front for the 774 lost in the same month (135 lost on the Eastern Front, 143 replacements; 610 lost on the Western Front, 166 replacements; 29 lost in Italy, six replacements). On the other hand, 490 Panthers out of 685 (350 produced in August, 335 in September) were sent as replacements for the 697 lost (132 lost on the Eastern Front, 186 replacements; 543 lost on the Western Front against 284 replacements; and 22 lost in Italy against 20 replacements). At this stage the Panther finally became the German main battle tank and, as such, it was used to create the new Panzer Brigade

A two-ton Ford Maultier (mule) half-track with a 20mm Flak 38 is taking up position in a prepared shelter; this was an improvement on the old one-ton self-propelled anti-aircraft SdKfz 10/4 which mounted the same weapon on the lighter Demag D 7 half-track chassis, giving it basic cross-country capabilities.

intended as a stopgap solution to the ever-worsening situation; at this stage the Western Front was seen as the most endangered area.

The figures available for November 1944 create a clearer picture of how the overall situation had changed in general for the Panzerwaffe; overall tank strength at the front (excluding the Tiger) was 2,768 tanks, which included 217 PzKpfw III out of the 523 still available in the German tank inventory (of the former 133 were on the Eastern Front, 35 on the Western Front and 49 in Italy), with no new ones produced in October–November, but with 22 lost in the same period. The bulk was provided by 1,457 PzKpfw IV out of the 1,525 in the inventory (759 on the Eastern Front, 532 on the Western Front and 166 in Italy), with 256 lost in October–November against 387 newly produced. Also there were 1,094 Panthers at the front against the 1,729 in the inventory, with 406 lost in October–November against 596 produced – the breakdown was as follows: 684 on the Eastern Front, 371 on the Western Front, 39 in Italy. Losses in December 1944, when the Ardennes offensive was unleashed, included 158 PzKpfw IV and 234 Panthers thus bringing the grand total in 1944 to 3,105 PzKpfw IV and 2,680 Panthers lost, of which only a few (294 PzKpfw IV and 110 Panthers) were eventually recovered and made operational again. Worth noting, the actual losses amounted to about 96 per cent of the yearly production of the PzKpfw IV and to about 71 per cent of that of the Panther. Without any chance of recovery, in January 1945 there was a belated attempt to fully reorganize the Panzerwaffe and an emergency Panzer production programme was laid out, according to which production of the PzKpfw IV was to last until April with 250 models produced every month, while 200 Panzerjäger IV/70 were to be produced in February and 250 thereafter, with it eventually replacing the PzKpfw IV in the production lines in May. Even the Panther was to have a limited life; 275 were to be produced in February and 290 in March and April, until production was to be halted in May. The only AFV to be produced in large quantities was now the Jagdpanzer 38, with an output of some 500 samples per month. As a matter of fact 438 PzKpfw IV and 507 Panthers were produced until April 1945 while another 53 PzKpfw IV and 57 Panthers were recovered in January 1945, when losses of both types were respectively 287 and 237. On 10 April 1945 the German tank inventory (field army only) still included 157 PzKpfw III, 468 PzKpfw IV and Jagdpanzer IV/70 (793 PzKpfw IV and 434 Jagdpanzer IV/70 on 15 March 1945) and 499 Panthers (954 on 15 March). The breakdown was as follows: on the Eastern Front 17

Towed anti-tank guns were still largely in use with the Panzer Divisions and, in early 1944, in many cases they still equipped at least one company of the Panzerjäger Abteilung. An SdKfz 11 Hanomag H KL 6 three-ton tractor, with interesting mottled camouflage, is towing a PAK somewhere in Belgium.

The Panzerjäger – here an abandoned SdKfz 138 Panzerjäger 38 (t) Ausf M – became obsolete in 1944 not only because of their characteristics (being lightly armoured, open-topped gun carriers) but also because they were to be replaced by the heavier Jagdpanzer. This is the last version of the Panzerjäger, produced up to May 1944.

PzKpfw III, 324 PzKpfw IV and Jagdpanzer IV/70 (603 PzKpfw IV and 357 Jagdpanzer IV/70 on 15 March), 446 Panthers (776 on 15 March); on the Western Front 13 PzKpfw IV and Jagdpanzer (59 PzKpfw IV and 77 Jagdpanzer IV/70 on 15 March) plus 29 Panthers (152 on 15 March), in Italy 53 PzKpfw III, 124 PzKpfw IV and Jagdpanzer (131 PzKpfw IV on 15 March), 24 Panthers (26 on 15 March); in Denmark and Norway 87 PzKpfw III and 7 PzKpfw IV. By then the Panzerwaffe had already lost the impressive number of 4,706 PzKpfw III, 7,636 PzKpfw IV and 5,629 Panthers since the beginning of the war, to say nothing of all the other light and heavy tanks.

From 1943 the assault gun, the Sturmgeschütz, became more and more important and was used in a wide variety of roles other than that originally intended for it, which was support for the infantry. Eventually it was used either as a tank-hunter or rarely as a replacement for tanks in the Panzer Sturmgeschütz Regiment (actually formed only with the 14, 16 and 24. Panzer Divisions). In 1943 production of the new, 75mm L/48 gun-armed Sturmgeschütz III stood at 3,011 plus 204 of the 105mm gun-armed Sturmhaubitze 42 (assault howitzer); figures for 1944 were respectively 3,849 and 903, while up to May 1945 some 1,038 Sturmgeschütz III and 98 Sturmhaubitze were still built. At the same time a new Sturmgeschütz IV based on the PzKpfw IV's body was developed, with 30 models built in 1943 plus 1,009 in 1944 and 127 in 1945 (along with 70, 215 and 25 of the 150mm gun-armed Sturmpanzer IV). The inventory in August 1943 included 1,573 Sturmgeschütz III plus 140 armed with the 75mm L/24 and 148 Sturmhaubitzen; of these 866 Sturmgeschütz III plus 56 Sturmhaubitzen were on the Eastern Front, while another 168 were in Italy. In January 1944 the inventory included 1,945 Sturmgeschütz III and IV (plus 193 obsolete StuG III) and 97 Sturmhaubitzen; the figures for June were 2,804 StuG III and IV (plus 207 obsolete StuG III, now probably only used for training) and 272 StuH. In January there were 1,875 Sturmgeschütz on the Eastern Front (though only 743 were operational), 223 in the West and 141 in Italy; in June only 250-odd StuG III were on the Eastern Front (though the figure does not include independent Stug units) while another 310 Sturmgeschütze and Jagdpanzer were on the Western Front (about 230 in France and Belgium with the Panzer and Panzergrenadier Divisions). The striking contrast between the inventory and field deployment is not only the consequence of different calculation methods, but also reveals the growing importance the Sturmgeschütz played on the battlefield; overall losses were 1,566 StuG III and IV plus 71 StuH in 1943 and 3,555 StuG III and IV plus 437 StuH in 1944, which amounted to 52 and 92 per

Although production started in January 1940, the Sturmgeschütz entered mass production only in early 1943 with the last Ausf G version, of which 7,720 examples were produced until March 1945. Its 75mm L/48 gun was the same used by the new Jagdpanzer IV/70, though the Sturmgeschütz needed appliqué armour.

cent of the yearly production in 1943 and 1944 of both the StuG III and IV. Worth noting, the odd 50 StuG reported in June 1944 by the five Panzer Divisions equipped with them became about 120–150 with a dozen or so Panzer Divisions in November, without taking attachments into account. Still, in November 1944 there were 1,687 Sturmgeschütze in the field (729 operational, probably all types) plus another 496 being delivered; the breakdown was 1,327 on the Eastern Front, 169 on the Western Front and 191 in Italy. The January 1945 Panzer emergency programme envisaged the construction of 400 Stug III plus 70 StuG IV per month from February through to April, when production was to be halted. On 10 April 1945 there were 1,036 StuG III and 282 StuG IV at the front, mostly (811 and 219) on the Eastern Front, in Italy (123 and 16), on the Western Front (45 and 40) and in Denmark and Norway (39 and 7).

Like the Sturmgeschütz, the Panzerjäger saw not only growing use and importance, but also several improvements. Production of the 75mm PAK 40 gun-armed Marder III on PzKpfw 38 (t) chassis saw an output of 975 samples between April 1943 and May 1944, while production of the lighter Marder II on PzKpfw II chassis had been halted in June 1943. Clearly a stopgap solution, the Marder was no longer a suitable tank-hunter in 1944 because of both inadequate armour and weaponry; a suitable replacement was found in the development of the StuG IV which, with a new body, turned into the first variant of the Jagdpanzer IV SdKfz 162. (The change of designation from Panzerjäger to Jagdpanzer –literally 'tank hunter' and 'hunter tank' – denoted not only the switch from the open-topped to the fully armoured vehicle, but also a change from the mainly defensive role played by the former and the offensive role the latter was to play.) Still armed with the 75mm L/48 gun, some 769 samples were produced in January to November 1944 though, since August, production of the new Panzer IV/70 (in the two versions V and A, the latter with higher silhouette) had started on the same body but with improved armour (80mm as opposed to 60mm) and weaponry, this time a 75mm PAK 42 L/70. 930 Panzer IV/70 (V) were built up to March 1945, plus another 278 Panzer IV/70 (A). The Panzerjäger not only served as a suitable replacement for the Jagdpanzer, but also as a replacement for the PzKpfw IV itself, especially when the new Jagdpanzer 38 (t) 'Hetzer' SdKfz 138/2 was developed (again using the PzKpfw 38 (t) chassis); production was started in April 1944, with some 2,584 examples produced until May 1945 (2,849 according to some sources) and first delivery to units came in July. With its lighter armour and weaponry (60mm, and 75mm PAK 39 L/48), it was actually more suitable as a tank-hunter than the Jadgpanzer IV, the latter being replaced in its role of heavy tank-hunter by the Jagdpanther and eventually the Jagdtiger. Most important of all, the 'Hetzer' provided a much-needed replacement for the towed 75mm PAK guns, the most widely used anti-tank gun of which some 9,613 examples (PAK 97/38, 39 and 40) were produced in 1943, when production of the 50mm PAK 38 was halted. In spite of the impressive production figures in 1944, 15,548 examples of the PAK 97/38, 39 and 40, losses were such there was no chance to replenish them. In 1943 some 1,854 50mm PAK 38 and 2,266 75mm PAK 40, 41 and 97/38 were lost, followed in 1944 by another 2,410 PAK 38 and 7,540 75mm PAK.

The enemy tank threat (in 1944 the Red Army and Allied forces had something like 50,000 tanks and AFVs) clearly could not be met by German AFVs alone since infantry, Panzergrenadiers in particular, had been lacking suitable anti-tank weapons from the early war years. A first solution was the development, from captured American gear, of the Raketen Panzer Büchse 54 (rocket anti-tank rifle) better known as Panzerschreck (tank terror) or simply Ofenrohr (stovepipe), an 88mm rocket projector which never became popular amongst the troops. Intended for use by the purposely formed Panzer Zerstörungs Trupp, each one equipped with three of them, the first 242 Panzerschreck reached the front in October 1943; only in January 1944 was the maximum figure of 21,141 reached amongst field units. The need for specific training and the many intricacies of the new weapon apparently were more than a hurdle; in spring 1944 the Panzerschreck practically disappeared from the organization charts and only returned in November, though in September there were 79,609 examples in use by field troops. In spite of the production of some 289,151 examples up to April 1945, the Panzerschreck never saw widespread use, in contrast to the much better-known Panzerfaust (armoured fist), a single-shot anti-tank rocket projector developed from the early version called the Faustpatrone (armoured bullet). From summer 1943, some 1,554,200 Faustpatrone and 6,700,100 Panzerfaust were produced up until the end of the war and, unlike the Panzerschreck, were widely used, with about 41,000 rounds reported fired in 1943, 2 million-plus reported fired in 1944 and 5,300,000-plus reported fired only in January–February 1945. Their effectiveness is another kettle of fish; the figures shown for the early months of 1944 on the Eastern Front are not representative of the actual effectiveness of German portable anti-tank weapons, which would prove deadlier later in the same year in the confined battle areas of North-West Europe and at the German border. Yet the widespread availability and actual use of the Panzerfaust should not be exaggerated, since the weapon still required not only a trained (and skilled) soldier to fire it against a tank at close range – less than 100m – but an even better-trained, skilled and luckier one to achieve a critical hit.

Portable anti-tank weapons were not the only improvement in infantry weaponry (the most notable one being the introduction of the automatic assault rifle Sturmgewehr 44 which, like the Panzerfaust, provided a useful model for Soviet post-war weapons). The Panzer Divisions in particular enjoyed for the very first time a wide availability of half-tracked – fully, partly or unarmoured – vehicles, which were now used also for combat support and not just as armoured personnel carriers. As early as November 1943 a Panzer Division would have, according to its war establishment charts, 28 unarmoured SdKfz 10/4 with a 20mm Flak 38, 13 semi-armoured SdKfz 7/1 with a 20mm, four-barrelled Flakvierling 38/1 and 233 armoured SdKfz 251, plus 64 lighter SdKfz 250. Of these, 47 were APCs SdKfz 251/1 (along with 22 SdKfz 250/1 performing the same role), another five SdKfz 251/4 were used as tractors and ammunitions carriers, and 42 were SdKfz 251/7 engineer vehicles. There were 47 radio and command

Street combat in a French or Belgian town close to the German border, autumn 1944. Note on the left the NCO and the soldier armed with the Sturmgewehr 44 and, in the centre, the Panzergrenadier with an Army camouflaged smock carrying a Panzerfaust. The heavy use of foliage on the StuG IV is rather curious in this setting.

A 150mm schwere Infanterie Geschütz (heavy infantry gun) selbstfahrlafette SdKfz 138/1 Ausf H 'Grille' (cricket) of Panzer Lehr Division's Panzergrenadier Regiment 901 or 902. The '9' on the hull suggests the photo was taken in late 1944, after the Fla Kompanien were disbanded and their number taken by the IG.

SdKfz 251/3 (plus two SdKfz 250/3) and another 22 telephone exchange vehicles (17 SdKfz 251/11, two SdKfz 251/19 and three SdKfz 250/2), plus 14 observation vehicles SdKfz 250/5. Support vehicles included a dozen mortar carriers (eight SdKfz 251/2, four SdKfz 250/7), 42 20mm gun-armed vehicles (16 SdKfz 250/9 with turret, 26 SdKfz 251/17), eight 37mm gun-armed SdKfz 251/10, 21 75mm gun-armed vehicles (18 SdKfz 251/9, three SdKfz 250/8) and six flamethrower-equipped SdKfz 251/16. The inventory also included seven SdKfz 251/8 armoured ambulances. These figures proved to be somewhat optimistic because some vehicles, like the SdKfz 251/17, either had not yet entered production or were in short supply. Nevertheless, the 1944 establishment charts brought some minor changes; the overall number of armoured half-tracks was increased and there was some shuffling due to availability. There were now 243 SdKfz 251 and 59 SdKfz 250; the breakdown included 57 APCs SdKfz 251/1 and 25 SdKfz 250/1 plus 37 engineer SdKfz 251/7 (SdKfz 251/4 being replaced by the 251/1), while command and communications vehicles included 50 SdKfz 251/3 (48 in November 1944), 15 SdKfz 251/11 (14 in November 1944), two SdKfz 251/19 plus 13 observation SdKfz 250/5, with both the SdKfz 250/2 and 3 no longer in use. Mortar carriers now stood at 20 (17 SdKfz 251/2 and 3 SdKfz 250/7), while 20mm gun-armed vehicles increased to 48 (still 16 SdKfz 250/9 plus 32 SdKfz 251/17); the SdKfz 251/10 was no longer in use, but there were now 22 75mm gun-armed vehicles (20 SdKfz 251/9 and 2 SdKfz 250/8) and the customary six SdKfz 251/16 flamethrowers were retained, along with the seven SdKfz 251/8 armoured ambulances. The unarmoured, 20mm gun-armed SdKfz 10/4 were now reduced to four, while the 13 SdKfz 7/1 had turned into nine 20mm four-barrelled Flakvierling 38/1-armed SdKfz 7/1 plus three 37mm Flak 43/1-armed SdKfz 7/2. Overall production of the SdKfz 251 sharply increased with 4,258 examples produced in 1943 and 7,785 in 1944, plus another 1,016 produced in 1945; on the other hand, production of the lighter SdKfz 250 declined from 2,895 in 1943 to 1,701 in 1944 and 269 in 1945. Eight SdKfz 250/8 were produced in 1943 compared with 10 in 1944 and 51 in 1945 (hardly capable of satisfying the need), while 324 reconnaissance SdKfz 250/9 were produced in 1943 compared with 318 in 1944 and 154 in 1945 – a vehicle badly needed to make good the lack of armoured cars. Production of some variants of the SdKfz 251 was as follows: 452 SdKfz 251/9 in 1943, 686 in 1944 and three in 1945; 231 SdKfz 251/10 in 1943 (production was halted); 338 SdKfz 251/16 in 1944 and nine in 1945; 121 SdKfz 251/17 in 1944 and 90 in 1945 (also 311 SdKfz 251/21 armed with three 20mm guns were produced in 1944, 76 in 1945, while 40 75mm PAK gun-armed SdKfz 251/22 were produced in 1944, plus another 228 in 1945). As these figures show, in spite of the increased overall availability of armoured half-tracks (though mostly used as APCs, engineer, command and communication vehicles) there also was clearly a perennial shortage of some of the most important – at least according to war establishments – support types like the SdKfz 251/17 and 16 (the latter intended to replace the Flamm Panzer III, itself produced in a very limited quantity: 100 in 1943), while the production rate of the 75mm gun-armed SdKfz 251/9 could not make good the almost non-existent production of its lighter counterpart, the SdKfz 250/8, and the concurrent shortage of the 75mm gun-armed armoured cars SdKfz 233 and 234/3.

The low production figures of the SdKfz 250, armed either with a 20mm or a 75mm gun, proved unable to counter the declining availability of armoured cars, as intended; the 1943 Panzer Division still required two SdKfz 261 light radio armoured cars in the motorized Panzergrenadier Regiment plus some other 12 light, four-wheeled, 20mm gun-armed SdKfz 222 and six four-wheeled SdKfz 223 light radio armoured cars in the Panzer Aufklärungs Abteilung, along with the heavy eight-wheeled ones (three 20mm-gun armed SdKfz 231, three radio SdKfz 232 and six 75mm gun-armed SdKfz 233). Production of the four-wheeled armoured cars practically ceased in 1943 with 306 examples of the SdKfz 221, 222 and 223 (the last 21 were produced in 1944) plus 76 examples of the SdKfz 260/261. Likewise, production of the eight-wheeled SdKfz 231 and 232 was halted in 1943 with the last 200 examples, while the 100 examples of the SdKfz 233 produced in 1943 were followed by the last 56 the following year. The new generation of eight-wheeled armoured cars had quite a troublesome birth; after the initial order in August 1940 it took three years of trials and tribulations to produce a 50mm, turret gun-armed, new armoured car designated the SdKfz 234/2 'Puma'. The first seven models were delivered in 1943, but soon the requirements changed and the forthcoming production of the SdKfz 234 series requested it to be armed with either a 20mm gun in the reconnaissance role or a 75mm gun in the support role. Therefore, production of the SdKfz 234/2 was cut short (94 examples produced in 1944) while the new 20mm gun-armed SdKfz 234/1 was delivered from June 1944, with 163 examples produced during the year plus another 37 in 1945. Only 88 examples of the 75mm gun-armed support SdKfz 234/3 were produced in 1944, which was eventually followed by the 75mm PAK gun-armed SdKfz 234/4 (25 were produced in 1944, 73 in 1945). Such a failure severely curtailed armoured car allowances in the Panzer Divisions; thus, while the April 1944 establishment still required thirteen SdKfz 234/1 and three SdKfz 234/3, the November one only required eight SdKfz 234/1 and seven SdKfz 234/3. With production focused on the Panzer and Panzerjäger, it was certainly hard to keep up with any other requirements, no matter how important these were for the Panzer Divisions.

Support armoured half-tracks and armoured cars were not the only items in short supply in the last years of war; the need to counter Allied air power, especially close air support which in 1943 destroyed many of the 9,357 AFVs lost by German armed forces (losses in 1942 were 3,301), highlighted the need for a Panzer Regiment equipped with a suitable armoured, fully tracked anti-aircraft vehicle. Once more, production of the Panzers took priority and in October 1943 Hitler halted the development of a PzKpfw IV chassis-based Flakpanzer, preferring instead that based on the chassis of the PzKpfw 38 (t). The result was the 20mm Flak 38-armed Flakpanzer 38 (SdKfz 140), which dramatically lacked firepower; 87 examples were produced in 1943 and 54 in 1944. Production of the first, real Flakpanzer on the PzKpfw IV chassis (the most suitable for carrying heavier weapons) started only in July 1944; the first attempt was the Flakpanzer IV 'Möbelwagen', at first equipped with the 20mm, four-barrelled Flakvierling 38/1 and subsequently armed with the 37mm Flak 43. Since this solution proved unsatisfactory, a new 20mm, four-barrelled Flakvierling 38/1 on a turret mount-equipped Flakpanzer IV 'Wirbelwind' was made by conversion of the PzKpfw IV

Enemy half-tracks compared on the battlefield; a heavily camouflaged SdKfz 251 (apparently towing a gun) passes by a burned-out American M3A1, which was its counterpart in use by Allied forces. The main difference between the German and the American model is that more than 41,000 examples were built of the latter.

tank bodies sent back for refitting. This too was undergunned, and so the 37mm Flak 43-armed 'Ostwind' version was subsequently produced. Production was always limited, with 205 examples of the 'Möbelwagen' in 1944 plus 35 more in 1945, 100 examples of the 'Wirbelwind' in 1944 plus 6 others in 1945, and 15 examples of the 'Ostwind' produced in 1944, plus 28 in 1945. The low rates of production seems to have luckily matched the low rate of losses; only 91 Flakpanzer of all types were lost in 1944 plus another 22 in January 1945. On 15 March 1945 there were still 159 Flakpanzer in service – 97 on the Eastern Front, 41 on the Western Front and 21 in Italy.

There seems to have been only a single case in which production of the Panzers did not take priority over the development of a Panzer chassis-based weapon that was not intended to carry another anti-tank weapon: that of self-propelled artillery. In 1943 a suitable solution was found for providing the Panzergrenadier Regiment with an efficient, and widely available, self-propelled Infanterie Geschütz, an infantry gun capable of providing close, heavy fire support. The first attempts – comprising the 38 examples of the schwere Infanterie Geschütz-armed PzKpfw I in 1940, and the dozen examples of the leichte Infanterie Geschütz-armed PzKpfw II produced in 1941–42 – had ended in failure. However, in February 1943 the first examples of the 150mm schwere Infanterie Geschütz 33-armed SdKfz 138/1 'Grille', based on the PzKpfw 38 (t) chassis, were delivered. The first batch of 91 examples of the H series (with the gun in a forward position) were followed by the new M series, which carried more ammunition (18 rounds as opposed to 15). All in all, 224 examples of the 'Grille' were produced in 1943, followed by another 138 in 1944 and a further 17 in 1945. The greatest innovation was, however, the development of the self-propelled howitzer carriers 'Wespe' and 'Hummel', which first provided the Panzer Divisions with the close, heavy and mobile fire support that had always been missing. Based on the PzKpfw II chassis, the SdKfz 124 'Wespe' carried a 105mm leichte Feldhaubitze 18 and proved so successful that from February 1943 all PzKpfw II chassis were ordered to be developed in this manner. The production figures are not clear; apparently between 662 and 753 'Wespe' were produced between February 1943 and July 1944, together with another 156 ammunition carriers. This carried 90 more rounds (the 'Wespe' only had 32) and, if needed, could be equipped on the field with the leichte Feldhaubitze. The heavier 150mm schwere Feldhaubitze 18-armed, next of kin to the 'Wespe' was the SdKfz 165 'Hummel' based on the lengthened chassis of the PzKpfw III/IV. Production was started in February 1943 and during the same year some 368 examples were delivered, followed by another 289 in 1944 and by 57 in 1945, plus 157 ammunition carriers – this was apparently not enough, since in 1944 their number was curtailed from three to two for each battery. No data concerning losses is available.

Interior view of the turret of a leichte Panzerspähwagen (light armoured car) SdKfz 222. In November 1943 a Panzer Aufklärungs Abteilung was still meant to have 12 of them and, though they disappeared from organization charts in April 1944, they were much appreciated and remained in use until the end of the war.

Command, control, communications and intelligence

The German command system

The German command system was rooted in the principles of 'Auftragstaktik', which is the basic notion of mission command. The system was quite simple; commanders were not told how to attain their objective (the overarching principle of the 'top down' command system) but were rather told what their objective was, then it was their choice how to attain it using available forces. The system worked at every level, and it was especially suited to fast, mobile units like the Panzer Divisions. At divisional level, the system was developed to fit the actual breakdown of the Panzer Divisions on the field, namely different combat groups. Until 1941, combat groups (Kampfgruppen) were the natural evolution of the march groups (Marschgruppen) built around the main components of a division, particularly the Panzer and the Schützen (later Panzergrenadier) Regiment. After the defeats of winter 1941/42 the use of Kampfgruppen changed to meet the new requirements of the battlefield; while in attack their role did not change, in defence they would be used either to hold portions of the front or to promptly counterattack enemy breakthroughs. Therefore, the Kampfgruppe turned into a smaller version of the Panzer Division, that was easier to handle; units at regimental/battalion level, mostly infantry, were strengthened using elements drawn from other units like the Panzer Regiment, the Panzer Aufklärungs and Panzerjäger Abteilung, the Panzer Pionier Bataillon and the Panzer Artillerie Regiment. This enabled them to face even stronger, armoured enemy forces. The system evolved in 1943–44 when the Kampfgruppe became the main tactical combat component of the Panzer Divisions on the battlefield; the command system evolved accordingly, while tactical doctrine was adapted during the last years of war.

Following the battle of Kursk the German Army, and the Panzer Divisions, were mainly forced into defensive warfare, even if this did not mean an end to offensive actions. In fact, offensive action was deemed the best tactical solution

The Sturmgeschütz IV SdKfz 167 entered production in December 1943; it was simply developed by adding the StuG III superstructure to the chassis of the PzKpfw IV with a few variations (like the lengthened driver's compartment). More than 1,100 examples were produced up to the end of the war.

A mixed Kampfgruppe column on the move, on the Eastern Front, winter 1943/44. Behind the SdKfz 251 in the foreground, carrying either Panzergrenadiers or Panzer Pioniere, follows a line of 105mm SdKfz 124 Wespe (self-propelled guns), which is followed by a Panzerbeobachtung III (tank observation vehicle).

in every case, thus enemy attacks and breakthroughs had to be dealt with using a rigid defence and counterattacks. The rigid defence system was based on a simple concept: units deployed on the front line were required to hold their positions regardless of any enemy breakthrough; this way the enemy attack would be broken into a series of isolated drives against which German counterattacks would be promptly unleashed. These counterattacks, led by the Panzer Divisions, were moulded by the basic concepts of German doctrine: swift action, concentration of forces, manoeuvre and encirclement, which led to the eventual annihilation of enemy forces. However, from mid-1943 onwards, the lack of forces and supplies compelled the Germans to switch to elastic defence, which was not as costly as the rigid one in terms of losses. Ground could be lost to the attacker, though every attempt to break through was to be halted using a blocking position, until the counterattack prevented any further attempt to advance by the enemy. Organization of the defence lines was changed; the forward defence line was formed by a series of outposts, intended only to fight rearguard actions aimed at delaying the enemy advance, while in the rear area a main line of resistance was created using anti-tank artillery. The Panzer Division counterattack was then intended either to regain the ground lost or to prevent further breakthroughs on the main line of resistance.

The use of Kampfgruppen and the command system

The use of regimental Kampfgruppen was practically the norm in 1943–44 for the Panzer Divisions. Generally speaking, these were built around the main elements according to their degree of motorization. Thus, the main Kampfgruppe would be formed around the Panzer unit (Regiment or Abteilung), along with any other available SPW-mounted Panzergrenadier, Aufklärungs and Pionier unit plus the self-propelled units from both the Panzer Artillerie Regiment and the Panzerjäger Abteilung. Other Kampfgruppen were formed from other units, mainly motorized infantry with anti-tank and artillery support. The example of Kampfgruppe von Waldenburg of the 24. Panzer Division, formed in early May 1944 around Panzergrenadier Regiment 26 and used to meet the Soviet breakthrough at Targul–Frumos, gives a detailed insight into the actual organization. Since the division had only a single Panzer Abteilung (III./Panzer Regiment 24, later II) and three Panzergrenadier Bataillone, the remnants of its Panzergrenadier Regiment 21 merged together in the II. Bataillon in January 1944, only two Kampfgruppen could be formed. The leading, armoured one was formed around the Stab of PzGrenRgt 26 with its I. Bataillon, which had three SPW mounted companies plus the regimental Stabs Kompanie (or Schwadron, as they were called by the division), the 9. schwere Infanterie Geschütz and the 10. Fla Kompanie. To make good the lack of infantry, Panzer Aufklärungs Abteilung 24 was added with its 1. Panzerspäh Kompanie (with 22 armoured cars) plus its motorized and armoured heavy company. III./Panzer Regiment 24 was the armoured component of the Kampfgruppe with three PzKpfw IV and Sturmgeschütz-equipped companies, while the self-propelled I./Panzer Artillerie Regiment offered support with its two companies, one equipped with the Hummel and one with the 150mm Brummbär assault howitzer. All in all, the Kampfgruppe had four armoured companies (one with armoured cars) and four infantry companies, plus three mixed heavy companies (with a total of three PAK, two Kanone, one infantry and two Pionier platoons) plus four Infanterie Geschütz batteries, three Fla ones and two of self-propelled artillery.

Clearly such a Kampfgruppe suffered from a lack of infantry and relied heavily on firepower – a common occurrence at this stage of the war, which could lead to the failure of a counterattack, as happened at Salerno. Since late 1943 the Panzer Aufklärungs Abteilung was no longer used in its reconnaissance role but rather served as infantry, though it lacked the strength of the Panzergrenadier Bataillon. Most important of all, one of the shortcomings of this organization, soon experienced on the Western Front, was the concentration of large numbers of AFVs, which could easily fall prey to enemy aircraft. A solution was found in the development of a quite different Kampfgruppe, now built around single Panzergrenadier units (battalions or regiments) each one supported by Panzer, Panzerjäger and Pionier companies. Smaller Kampfgruppen were easier to handle and had more infantry, though their weakness in armour and firepower often left them unable to exploit their breakthroughs.

Changes in organization affected both the employment of the Kampfgruppe on the battlefield and the command system. From late 1943 the German Army suffered from an overall lack of vehicles and supplies, which greatly affected mobility and flexibility on the battlefield. Redeployment, at every level, was hampered and now difficult terrain, as at Salerno and Targul–Frumos, and enemy superiority (like that at St. Lo and in the Ardennes) prevented a prompt redeployment of those Kampfgruppe already engaged. The Germans were also no longer able to bring in reinforcements, both because of the lack of reserves and of supplies, which prevented follow-on units from keeping up with the pace of advance. A lack of adequate reconnaissance, mainly due to enemy air superiority, was also a major hurdle, though it is worth noting that the Panzer Divisions had already experienced similar shortcomings in the early stages of Operation Barbarossa, making them good only thanks to speed and flexibility. In 1943–44 the Panzer Divisions lost a good deal of their superiority in terms of both speed and flexibility and, though the Kampfgruppe system worked at the tactical level in defence and (to a limited extent) in attack, their weakness often made them unable to achieve any decisive result.

The command system was also affected. Until early 1944 the 'Auftragstaktik' system was still largely used. However, the system revealed its shortcomings that year, especially on the Western Front; the lack of strength and the impossibility of quickly redeploying units required better coordinated attacks and manoeuvres,

Officers are shown discussing the immediate situation and checking their maps, on the Eastern Front, winter 1943/44. The 'lead forward' concept saw many high-ranking officers moving with their units to meet the enemy, which enabled them to gain a first hand appreciation of the situation – though it often led to high casualties.

in which individual commanders were no longer allowed to follow their instinct. This was the only way to improve actual combat effectiveness on the field and to avoid surprises, while maintaining close control of the situation on the battlefield. Orders became more strict and more detailed, leaving less to the personal initiative of a Kampfgruppe commander; the time and the place of attack were given to him, though he was still left with the choice of how to deploy and lead his units. Good examples are given by the different situations experienced by the 24. Panzer Division at Targul–Frumos and by the Panzer Lehr at St. Lo. In the first case terrain prevented the two Kampfgruppen from manoeuvring after the initial deployment, thus denying flexibility. In the second case flexibility was denied by Allied air and ground superiority, which required coordination between the four different spearheads and also hampered any redeployment should one of the two main Kampfgruppen achieve a breakthrough. In the first case, the divisional commander decided to split his forces into two separate Kampfgruppen and to leave it to their commanders how best to deal with their objectives and with the situation on the battlefield. In the second case, the divisional commander laid down on his Kampfgruppe commanders both the timing and the place of the attack, since the lack of intelligence and Allied air superiority required a closer control of the situation on the battlefield. This denied the division any chance of exploiting the minor breakthrough that was achieved, dooming the attack as a whole.

Tighter control was also one of the consequences of the German communication system; this was mainly based on a pyramid-like structure which saw units directly linked to their superior HQ all the way up, from the single company to the divisional level. If the system actually worked to meet the needs of the units on the battlefield, though not without serious shortcomings (cases of friendly fire were common), it did not work at all when different units, above all different types of units, had to cooperate on the battlefield. Since the Panzer Divisions were no longer fighting in groups of sister units under a single corps headquarters but rather had to fight along with the infantry divisions already manning frontlines defences, problems were encountered with communications. It proved extremely difficult to establish a direct line of communication between units operating in quite different manners, even when they were neighbouring ones practically fighting shoulder to shoulder. Thus, since the 'pyramid' communication system mainly worked at divisional/corps level, the Panzer Divisions' HQs were required to exercise tighter control on their subordinate units since they were the only ones who could maintain a certain degree of communication between units from different divisions on the battlefield.

Men of an unknown Kampfgruppe are waiting for the order to move; generally speaking, the Panzer Divisions built their main Kampfgruppe using all of their available armoured units, such as the Panzers and half-track-mounted Panzergrenadier regiments, plus other armoured elements from artillery, engineer and recce units.

Unit status

The Panzerwaffe's chief problem following the battle of Kursk was the failure to conduct a major reorganization of its divisions. The divisions were reorganized piecemeal during lulls on the front, most often with some of their units (in particular Panzer, Panzerjäger and Panzer Aufklärungs Abteilungen) sent back to Germany to rest, refit and reorganize according to new establishments. Since most of the army's Panzer Divisions were on the Eastern Front, changes only occurred between 1943 and 1944; following the disbandment of 18. Panzer Division on 7 September 1943 (on the 30th it formed 18. Artillerie Division), the German Army was down to 22 Panzer Divisions, the same number as in summer 1941. In the meantime, in mid-October 1943 seven Waffen-SS Panzer Divisions were either reorganized as such or newly formed, thus altering the balance much in favour of the latter. The formation in early 1944 of the new Lehr and 116. Panzer Divisions allowed the army to partially regain the upper hand, at least until the crisis that followed during the summer of 1944. The Panzerwaffe never really recovered from the latter. A partial reorganization did follow during the autumn and winter of 1944–45, still in a piecemeal fashion, but full combat effectiveness was never recovered and every attempt eventually ended in failure. During the autumn new Panzer Korps (armoured corps) were formed using 'twin' Panzer Divisions, which had to give their supply and service units to the corps command, leaving the main task of fighting to the single division. The experiment was not only extremely limited, but also ended in failure, since the Germans were unfamiliar with this kind of organization. The last reorganization of spring 1945, which led to the 1945 Panzer Division, not only remained mostly on paper but also sanctioned the ultimate defeat of the Panzerwaffe, since now both Panzer and Panzergrenadier divisions had the same structure, their armoured element being reduced to a single Panzer Abteilung.

The process of reorganization is hard to chart. Some divisions are known to have been reorganized as 1943 Panzer Divisions between late 1943 and early 1944; both 1 and 14. Panzer Divisions started their reorganization in October–November 1943, followed by 2. Panzer (December 1943–January 1944), 3. Panzer (January 1944), 9. Panzer (March 1944) and 25. Panzer Division as late as May 1944. Most of these divisions were stationed on the Western Front after having been withdrawn from the east (to where, in some cases, they returned). Other divisions probably reorganized during the same period as well, mostly in a piecemeal fashion. Little later reorganization according to the 1944 Panzer Division establishment took place; at least a dozen Panzer Divisions (1, 4, 5, 7, 8, 9, 11, 12, 16, 17, 20 and Lehr) were ordered to reorganize in May–June 1944, followed by another nine in July–August (3, 6, 13, 14, 19, 23, 24, 25 and 116). The remaining ones followed suit in the autumn; 26. Panzer in August–September, 2. Panzer on 10 September and 21. Panzer Division on 11 October. In practice, the process took much longer than planned; at least eight divisions actually completed their reorganization only in the autumn (3, 13, 14 and 20. Panzer in September–October; 8, 9, 11 and Lehr Panzer in November), while another three did follow in winter (4 and 24. Panzer by January 1945, 25. Panzer Division until February 1945). Few of the divisions reorganized according to a new war establishment were at full strength; rather they would have implemented the new organization mostly at regimental/battalion level and the new KStN at company level. This is particularly true for the eight divisions which were ordered to adopt the new 1945 Panzer Division/Kampfgruppe organization in March–April 1945 (2, 7, 13, 16, 17, 25, 116 and FHH), plus all the divisions newly raised in the same year.

In spite of the attempt to reach uniformity, the divisions still had many organizational differences. In late 1943 at least three divisions already had a Begleit Kompanie or like (17 and 23, 24. Panzer Divisions had a Begleit Schwadron), and four others were formed between December 1943 (2. Panzer Division) and January–February 1944 (1, 7 and Lehr Panzer Divisions), followed by three others in March–April (9, 11 and 26. Panzer Divisions). The vast majority of the Begleit Kompanien would only have been formed in May–July 1944 (3, 4, 5, 6, 8, 12, 13, 19, 20, 25 and 116. Panzer Divisions), with a follow up in October (21. Panzer Division) and even in February 1945 (FHH; it is not certain whether 14 and 16. Panzer Divisions formed theirs). The situation was even worse for the Panzer Regiments, heavily affected by the reorganization and re-equipment with the new Panther tanks; delays in the process and the need to tackle crises on different fronts eventually imposed a major reshuffling of units, which not only added chaos to confusion, but also influenced the actual organization of the Panzer Divisions. Only four Panzer Divisions had their own Panther-equipped Abteilung back by the end of 1943: 1. Panzer (first equipped with PzKpfw IV, back in November), 11. Panzer (attached as Panzer Abteilung 52, rebuilt and back with the division in December), 16. Panzer (operational since October, first detached to other divisions until rejoining its parent one in December) and 23. Panzer Division, whose II./PzRgt 23 became operational in August only to join its parent division in September, before being rebuilt again in March 1944, and eventually rejoining the division in late June. Seven other Panzer Divisions had their Panther Abteilung back by August 1944: 2. Panzer in March, 4 and 5. Panzer in June (the latter rebuilt after it had been detached to another division from November 1943), 7 and 9. Panzer (July), 14 and 19. Panzer Division in August. Six did follow by the end of 1944 (20. Panzer in October; 116. Panzer in November; 3, 6 and 8. Panzer Division in December, the latter as a full Panther Abteilung after having been a mixed one). Only two joined their parent divisions in 1945: Panzer Lehr (used to form Panzer Brigade 113 and replaced by I./PzRgt 6, rebuilt and attached to other divisions until rebuilt again in December 1944, only to join the division in February 1945) and 17. Panzer Division, whose I./PzRgt 39 was formed from Panzer Brigade 103 on 15 March 1945.

Four Panther Abteilungen were detached to other units, never to rejoin their parent divisions (12 and 13. Panzer, whose I./PzRgt 4 was sent to Italy to face the Allied landings at Anzio and eventually became part of 26. Panzer Division; 24. Panzer whose I./PzRgt 24 was detached to the 116, 1 and 6. Panzer Divisions; 26. Panzer Division, whose I./PzRgt 26 was detached to 25. Panzer, Grossdeutschland and Brandenburg Divisions until being officially replaced by the already detached I./PzRgt 4. I./PzRgt Grossdeutschland, formed on 15 October 1943, went to the 116. Panzer Division on 6 May 1944 until being detached to the 6. Panzer Division early in June, eventually returning to its parent division on 13 December 1944). Three other Abteilungen were either never equipped with Panthers or never formed at all (21, 25 and FHH Panzer Divisions). Such an uneven organization, quite the contrary to what should have been achieved, was matched in the Panzer Flamm (flamethrowers) and Panzer Fla Zug; only seven of the former were actually formed with 1, 6, 11, 14, 16, 24 and 26. Panzer Divisions (all disappeared between late 1943 and early 1944, save for 26. Panzer's III./PzRgt 24, which retained its Panzer Flamm Zug until May 1944). Also, only nine Panzer Fla Züge seem to have been actually formed with 2, 21, 26 and Panzer Lehr Divisions in January 1944, followed by 6. Panzer (June), 9. Panzer (April), 11. Panzer (May), 19. Panzer (June) and 116. Panzer Divisions (April 1944). Unsurprisingly, most of these divisions fought on the Western Front. Several Panzer Abteilungen also had a mixed organization, to include two PzKpfw IV and two Sturmgeschütz companies (14. Panzer and 24. Panzer

Division's III, later II./PzRgt 36 and II./24 from summer 1943; 2. Panzer's II./PzRgt 3 and 9. Panzer Division's I./PzRgt 33 from November 1944; 116. Panzer Division's II./PzRgt 16 from December 1944), two PzKpfw IV and two Panther companies (8. Panzer's I./PzRgt 10 between August and November 1944; II./Panzer Lehr Regiment 130 from October 1944 and 21. Panzer Division's I./PzRgt 22 from November), or Sturmgeschütz and Panzer IV/70-equipped companies.

Table 4: Organization and unit numbers of the Panzer Divisions, 1943–44

Panzer Division	Panzer Rgt.	PzGren. Rgt.	Pz. Aufkl. Abt.	Panzerjäger Abt.	Pz. Artillerie Rgt.	H.Flak Art. Abt.	Pz. Pionier Btl.	PzD. Nachr. Abt.	FE Btl.	Services
1	1	1, 113	1	37	73	299	37	37	73	81
2	3	2, 304	2	38	74	273	38	38	74	82
3	6	3, 394	3	543	75	314	39	39	75	83
4	35	12, 33	4	49	103	290	79	79	103	84
5	31	13, 14	5	53	116	288	89	77	116	85
6	11	4, 114	6	41	76	298	57	82	76	57
7	25	6, 7	7	42	78	296	58	83	58	58
8	10	8 (98), 28	8	43	80	286	59	84	59	59
9	33	10, 11	9	50	102	287	86	85	102	60
11	15	110, 111	11	61	119	277	209	89	119	61
12	29	5, 25	12	2	2	303	32	2	2	2
13	4	66, 93	13	13	13	271	4	13	13	13
14	36	103, 108	14	4	4	276	13	4	4	4
16	2	64, 79	16	16	16	274	16	16	16	16
17	39	40, 63	17	27	27	297	27	27	27	27
18	18	52, 101	18	88	88	292	98	88	88	88
19	27	73, 74	19	19	19	272	19	19	19	19
20	21	59, 112	20	92	92	295	92	92	92	92
21	22	125, 192	21	200	155	305	220	200	200	200
23	23	126, 128	23	128	128	278	51	128	128	128
24	24	21, 26	24	40	89	283	40	86	89	40
25	9	146, 147	25	87	91	279	87	87	91	87
26	26	9, 67	26	51	93	304	93	93	93	93
116	16	60, 156	116	228	146	281	675	85	116	66
Lehr	130	901, 902	130	130	130	311	130	130	130	130
FHH	FHH	FHH, FHH	FHH	FHH	FHH	FHH	FHH	FHH	FHH	FHH

Notes:
8. Panzer Division: Panzergrenadier Regiment 98 from 20 November 1944
21. Panzer Division: Panzer Regiment 100 until 20 May 1944, then 22
25. Panzer Division: Heeres Flak Artillerie Abteilung 284 until 10 March 1944, then 279
26. Panzer Division: Panzerjäger Abteilung 51 formed on 16 October 1944
116. Panzer Division: Panzer Regiment 116 until 20 May 1944
Feldersatz Bataillon 146 until 8 June 1944
Panzer Lehr: until 1 April 1944 units were simply designated 'Lehr' (with Panzergrenadier Regiment Lehr 1 and 2), and from then onwards were designated 'Lehr' plus numbers as shown
FHH Feld Herrn Halle/Feldherrnhalle; it had one Panzergrenadier Regiment FHH and one Grenadier Regiment FHH

Table 5: Development of the Panzer Divisions' Panther Abteilung, 1943–45

PzDiv	Unit	Formed	Operational	Status
1.	I./PzRgt 1	5 March 43 22 October 43	(25 June 43) 16 November 43	First reorganization halted 25 June (with Pz IV to 1. PzDiv). Rebuilt with Panther, to 1. PzDiv
2.	I./PzRgt 3	27 July 43	5 March 44	From PzAbt 201, to 2. PzDiv
3.	I./PzRgt 6	6 August 43	26 January 44	To Lehr PzDiv 26 January to 27 September 44, then to 3. PzDiv from December 44
4.	II./PzRgt 35 / I./PzRgt 35	24 September 43	18 June 44	From III./PzRgt 15, became I./PzRgt 35 on 13 May 44. To 4. PzDiv.
5.	I./PzRgt 31	15 March 43	29 November 43	To 11. PzDiv, back to Germany January 44 to refit. To 5. PzDiv on 4 June 44
6.	I./PzRgt 11	1 April 43	16 March 44	To PzVbd Friebe, June to 8. PzDiv, on 25 August 44 to Germany to refit. On 8 December 44 to 6. PzDiv
7.	I./PzRgt 25	1 September 43	18 July 44	To 7. PzDiv
8.	I./PzRgt 10	30 August 44 27 November 44	8 September 44 25 December 44	To 8. PzDiv, mixed (two Panther Kp.). To 8. PzDiv as a full Panther Abteilung
9.	II./PzRgt 33	3 January 44		From PzAbt 51 to 9. PzDiv, rebuilt March–July 44
11.	I./PzRgt 15	6 February 43 19 August 43	July 43 5 December 43	From PzAbt 52 (formed from I./PzRgt 15, attached to division on 28 July), rebuilt to 11. PzDiv
12.	I./PzRgt 29	4 July 43 15 February 44	(15 Nov. 43) 5 September 44	First a static Panther Abt, rebuilt to PzBrig 112. Since January 45 (mixed Abt) to PzBrig 103, eventually to PzDiv Münchenberg
13.	I./PzRgt 4	5 May 43	24 January 44	From III./PzRgt 4 on 19 October 43, attached to 26. PzDiv became I./PzRgt 26 on 12 February 45
14.	I./PzRgt 36	3 August 43	18 August 44	To 14. PzDiv
16.	I./PzRgt 2	4 June 43	4 October 43	To 13 and 17. PzDiv, then 16. PzDiv in December 43
17.	I./PzRgt 39	17 Dec. 44	15 March 45	Formed from PzBrig. 103, to 17. PzDiv
19.	I./PzRgt 27	15 September 43	25 July 44	To 19. PzDiv on 1 August 44
20.	I./PzRgt 21	28 October 44		From PzBrig. 101, to 20.PzDiv (became II./PzRgt 21 on 30 December 44)
21.	II./PzRgt 22	28 July 44		Never equipped with tanks
23.	II./PzRgt 23	20 March 43 9 March 44	28 August 43 16 April 44	To 9. PzDiv, since 16 September to 23. PzDiv. Rebuilt, to 17 and 16. PzDiv; back to 23. PzDiv on 23 June
24.	I./PzRgt 24	3 August 43 25 November 44	4 July 44 17 January 45	To 116. PzDiv until 25 November 44. Rebuilt, to 1. PzDiv until 15 February 45; refit, to 6. PzDiv on 12 March 45 until 28 April
25.	I./PzRgt 9	3 November 44		*From PzBrig 104, from 13 February 45 a mixed Abt. – never equipped with Panthers*
26.	I./PzRgt 26	3 June 43 12 February 45	28 August 43	To 25. PzDiv until 22 October, refit and to PzGrenDiv GD on 3 January 44. Became 18 January 45 I./PzRgt Brandenburg. New I./PzRgt 26 from I./PzRgt 4
116.	I./PzRgt 116	29 June 44	5 September 44	To PzBrig 111 until 25 September 44, rebuilt to 116. PzDiv on 8 November 44
Lehr	I./PzRgt 130	28 July 44 25 September 44	5 September 44 early Dec. 44	To PzBrig 113 until 25 September. Rebuilt, to 1 and 23. PzDiv until 20 January 45. Rebuilt again, to PzDiv Lehr on 18 February 45
FHH	I./PzRgt FHH	27 November 44		*Mixed, to PzDiv FHH. Rebuilt 28 February 45 from PzAbt 208, never formed as a Panther Abteilung*

Panzergrenadier Regiments were no exception to such uneven organization. 17. Panzer Division had no armoured Panzergrenadier Bataillon at all while 23. Panzer Division had its I./PzGrenRgt 126 armoured only on paper. On the contrary 2, 21, Lehr and partly 25. Panzer Divisions had two or more armoured battalions; Lehr actually had four, at least until August and October 1944 (when respectively II./PzGrenRgt Lehr 901 and 902 were reorganized as motorized battalions), likewise 21. Panzer's I./PzGrenRgt 192 and 2. Panzer Division's I./PzGrenRgt 304 ceased to be armoured in October and November 1944 respectively (both 21. Panzer Division's Panzergrenadier Regiments were equipped with captured French vehicles). 25. Panzer Division's I./PzGrenRgt 146, armoured since September 1943, was joined by I./PzGrenRgt 147 which became armoured in November 1944 only to be disbanded in February 1945. At the end of 1943, or in early 1944, all the other Panzer Divisions had their own armoured battalion, some of which eventually reverted to motorized status late in 1944 (1 Panzer's I./PzGrenRgt 113; 3. Panzer's I./PzGrenRgt 3, motorized between August and October 1944; 4. Panzer's I./PzGrenRgt 12; 5. Panzer's I./PzGrenRgt 14; 6. Panzer's II./PzGrenRgt 114; 7. Panzer's II./PzGrenRgt 6; 8. Panzer's I./PzGrenRgt 8, with a single armoured company in November 1943 and fully armoured from January 1944; 9. Panzer's I./PzGrenRgt 10 plus one armoured company in PzGrenRgt 11 from September 1944; 11. Panzer's I./PzGrenRgt 110; 12. Panzer's I./PzGrenRgt 25 from January 1944; 13. Panzer's I./PzGrenRgt 66, no longer from February 1945; 14. Panzer's I./PzGrenRgt 103; 16. Panzer's II./PzGrenRgt 64; 19. Panzer's I./PzGrenRgt 74 from December 1943; 20. Panzer's II./PzGrenRgt 59 from October 1943; 24. Panzer's I./PzGrenRgt 26; 26. Panzer's I./PzGrenRgt 9; 116. Panzer's I./PzGrenRgt 60 and Feld Herrn Halle's I./PzGrenRgt FHH). Uniformity practically disappeared in the support companies of the Panzergrenadier Regiment; for example, in 1943 only the Infanterie Geschütz Kompanie was common, while all of the Fla Kompanie created in the regiments of 14 Panzer Divisions were disbanded from April 1944 and replaced with the newly formed Panzergrenadier Pionier Kompanie.

Between summer and winter 1943 there was a first reshuffling amongst the Panzer Divisions, some of which had been newly rebuilt after Stalingrad and the winter battles on the Eastern Front. In summer 1943 there were 15 divisions on the Eastern Front, plus the 18. Panzer Division which was disbanded on 7 September 1943; most were in the south (3, 6, 7, 9, 11, 13, 17, 19, 23), six in the centre (2, 4, 5, 8, 12, 20) and none in the north. Following the Allied invasion of Sicily, and the forecast of Italy's surrender, between July and August 16, 24 and 26. Panzer Divisions were sent to Italy and 1. Panzer Division was sent to the Balkans; of these, only 26. Panzer fought in Italy until the end of the war while the others went to the Eastern Front in October–November 1943: 1 (south), 16 (centre) and 24. Panzer (north), also joined by the 14. Panzer Division (rebuilt in France) and by the 25. Panzer Division (both south), which on 25 August 1943 was used to form Panzer Division Norwegen. That eventually enabled some worn-out divisions to be pulled out and sent to north-western Europe for rest and refit; 2. Panzer in December 1943, 9. Panzer in April 1944, 11. Panzer in April–May and 19. Panzer Division in June 1944. The latter was the only one to return to the Eastern Front in August, while all others joined the three divisions forming in France in view of the Allied invasion. These were the rebuilt 21. Panzer (formed 27 June 1943), the newly formed Panzer Lehr Division (6 January 1944, from 1 April its units were numbered 130) and the 116. Panzer Division (formed 30 March 1944 from the 16. Panzergrenadier Division and 179. Reserve Panzer Division). Also, having been all but destroyed in February 1944, 25. Panzer Division was rebuilt in Denmark on 1 July 1944 using the disbanded Panzer Division Norwegen. Between June and August 1944, when the German army suffered defeat on the Western and Eastern Fronts, there were six Panzer

Divisions in the West, 16 in the East (including 14. Panzer and 12. Panzer Division, the latter reorganized between March and June), one in Italy and one forming. All suffered heavily, losing a good deal of their combat effectiveness and, above all, their weapons and equipment. Moreover, since they could not be pulled out from the front a stopgap solution was found with the creation of the Panzer Brigade which, formed sometimes with units from the Panzer Divisions (both Panzer Brigade 103 and 104 originated from the 25. Panzer), were eventually absorbed by them during the last reorganization that took place in the autumn.

Between October and November 1944 several divisions were rebuilt and reorganized, mainly on the Western Front in view of the planned counteroffensive; in September, 25. Panzer Division was sent to the Eastern Front (to the Warsaw area), while on 27 November 16 and 17. Panzer Divisions together formed the XXIV. Panzer Korps. On 27 November Panzer Division Feld Herrn Halle was formed from the homonymous Panzergrenadier Division; intended to create Panzer Korps FHH along with 13. Panzer Division, it went to Budapest, where it was encircled and eventually destroyed in February 1945. A last reorganization started in February 1945 when 21. Panzer Division was pulled out from the front, rebuilt and sent to the East. On 3 February 14. Panzer Division was split into two Panzer Brigades and, during the month, five divisions were activated using replacement and school units: Holstein (1 February, disbanded 21 March), Jüteborg (20 February, 1 March absorbed by 16. Panzer Division), Schlesien (20 February, disbanded 21 March), and 232 and 233. Panzer Divisions (21 February). On 5 March Panzer Division Münchenberg was formed in Berlin and on the 31st the remnants of 13. Panzer Division were used to build Panzer Division FHH 2. On 4 April 1945 Panzer Division Clausewitz was formed and, on the 16th, 5. Panzer Division was disbanded in Courland, its remnants being absorbed by 233. Panzer Division. All the other Panzer Divisions disappeared a fortnight later.

A Panzergrenadier Gefreiter (corporal) discussing the tactical situation with a PzKpfw IV driver. The Germans had never developed a means of direct communication between tank commanders and the supporting infantry during combat (unlike the Americans, who installed external telephones on their tanks), and the only link was provided by command vehicle radios.

Index

References to illustrations are shown in **bold**.